汉英对照 |

十九大篇

19th National Congress
of the Communist
Party of China

中国关键词

KEYWORDS
TO
UNDERSTAND CHINA

权 威 解 读 当 代 中 国

中国外文出版发行事业局（CIPG）
当代中国与世界研究院（ACCWS）
中国翻译研究院（CATL）

新世界出版社
NEW WORLD PRESS

First Edition 2018

Compiled by
China International Publishing Group
Academy of Contemporary China and World Studies
China Academy of Translation

Translated by
Cai Lijian and Han Qingyue

English text edited by
David W. Ferguson and Xu Mingqiang

Cover designed by
He Yuting

ISBN 978-7-5104-6664-9

Published by
NEW WORLD PRESS
24 Baiwanzhuang Street, Beijing 100037, China

Distributed by
NEW WORLD PRESS
24 Baiwanzhuang Street, Beijing 100037, China
Tel: 86-10-68995968
Fax: 86-10-68998705
Website: www.nwp.com.cn
E-mail: nwpcd@sina.com

Printed in the People's Republic of China

《中国关键词：十九大篇》
图书编委会名单

19th National Congress of the Communist Party of China

Editorial Committee

INTRODUCTION
前 言

《中国关键词：十九大篇》多文种系列图书是“中国关键词多语对外传播平台”项目阶段性成果之一。

“中国关键词多语对外传播平台”是中国外文出版发行事业局、当代中国与世界研究院和中国翻译研究院联合组织实施的国家重点项目，主要围绕习近平新时代中国特色社会主义思想，进行中文词条专题编写、解读以及多语种编译，通过平面、网络和移动社交平台等多媒体、多渠道、多形态及时持续对外发布，旨在以国外受众易于阅读和理解的方式，阐释中国理念和中国思想，解读中国政策和中国道路。

为了使读者更全面、客观地了解党的十九大精神，《中国关键词》项目组联合中央相关部委、涉外新闻媒体、科研机构以及高等院校的研究及翻译专家，系统梳理、专题编写、编译出版了《中国关键词：十九大篇》中外对照多文种系列图书，涵盖中文、英语、法语、俄语、西班牙语、阿拉伯语、德语、葡语、意大利语、日语、韩语、越南语、印尼语、土耳其语、哈萨克语等 15 个语种。

由于能力及时间所限，在中文词条选择和编写时，难免挂一漏万，表述也可能存在偏颇；外文译文表达也可能多有不足，仅供阅读参考，欢迎读者指正。

讲故事需要“关键词”，讲好中国故事需要“中国关键词”。让我们用“中国关键词”点击中国、沟通世界。

Keywords to Understand China: the 19th National Congress of the Communist Party of China is a selection of the “China Keywords” entries included in an eponymous multilingual platform.

The “China Keywords” platform, a national-level project undertaken by the China International Publishing Group, Academy of Contemporary China and World Studies and China Academy of Translation, offers expert interpretation of Xi Jinping Thought on Socialism with Chinese Characteristics for a New Era through multiple means of the media, and serves an international audience as a window into China’s political thinking, policies, and path of development.

Complied jointly by scholars and translators from relevant ministries, the media, academies, and universities, it provides timely updates in Chinese as well as in Arabic, English, French, German, Indonesian, Italian, Japanese, Kazakh, Korean, Portuguese, Russian, Spanish, Turkish, and Vietnamese.

We hope that these “China Keywords” will help build a bridge of understanding between China and the rest of the world.

CONTENTS
目 录

新时代中国共产党的历史使命 · The New Era: The Historic Mission of the Communist Party of China

决胜全面建成小康社会，开启全面建设社会主义现代化国家新征程 · Completing the Building of a Moderately Prosperous Society in All Respects

贯彻新发展理念，建设现代化经济体系 · Applying a New Vision of Development and Developing a Modernized Economy

健全人民当家做主制度体系，发展社会主义民主政治 · Improving the System of Institutions Through Which the People Run the Country and Developing Socialist Democracy

新时代中国特色社会主义思想和基本方略

Principles and Basic Policies for Promoting Socialism with Chinese Characteristics for a New Era

中国特色社会主义进入新时代

改革开放之初，中国共产党发出了走自己的路、建设中国特色社会主义的伟大号召。从那时起，中国共产党团结带领全国各族人民不懈奋斗，推动中国经济实力、科技实力、国防实力、综合国力进入世界前列，推动中国国际地位实现前所未有的提升，中国共产党的面貌、中国的面貌、中国人民的面貌、中国军队的面貌、中华民族的面貌发生了前所未有的变化，中华民族正以崭新姿态屹立于世界东方。

经过长期努力，中国特色社会主义进入了新时代，这是中国发展新的历史方位。作出这个重大政治判断，是一项关系全局的战略考量。中国特色社会主义进入新时代，意味着近代以来久经磨难的中华民族迎来了从站起来、富起来到强起来的

Socialism with Chinese Characteristics Has Entered a New Era

In the early days of reform and opening up, the Party made a clarion call for us to take a path of our own and build socialism with Chinese characteristics. Since that time, the Party has united and led all the Chinese people in a tireless struggle, propelling China into a leading position in terms of economic and technological strength, defense capabilities, and composite national strength. China's international standing has risen as never before. Our Party, country, people, armed forces, and nation have changed in ways without precedent. The Chinese nation, with an entirely new posture, now stands tall and firm in the East.

With decades of hard work, socialism with Chinese characteristics has crossed the threshold into a new era. This is a new historic juncture in China's development.

This is what socialism with Chinese characteristics entering a new era means: The Chinese nation, which since modern times began had endured so much for so long, has achieved a tremendous transformation: It has stood up, grown rich, and is becoming strong; it has come to embrace the brilliant prospects of rejuvenation. It means that scientific socialism is full of vitality in

伟大飞跃，迎来了实现中华民族伟大复兴的光明前景；意味着科学社会主义在21世纪的中国焕发出强大生机活力，在世界上高高举起了中国特色社会主义伟大旗帜；意味着中国特色社会主义道路、理论、制度、文化不断发展，拓展了发展中国家走向现代化的途径，给世界上那些既希望加快发展又希望保持自身独立性的国家和民族提供了全新选择模式，为解决人类问题贡献了中国智慧和中国方案。

这个新时代，是承前启后、继往开来、在新的历史条件下继续夺取中国特色社会主义伟大胜利的时代，是决胜全面建成小康社会、进而全面建设社会主义现代化强国的时代，是全国各族人民团结奋斗、不断创造美好生活、逐步实现全体人民共同富裕的时代，是全体中华儿女勠力同心、奋力实现中华民族伟大复兴中国梦的时代，是我国日益走近世界舞台中央、不断为人类作出更大贡献的时代。中国特色社会主义进入新时代，在中华人民共和

21st-century China, and that the banner of socialism with Chinese characteristics is now flying high and proud for all to see. It means that the path, the theory, the system, and the culture of socialism with Chinese characteristics have kept developing, blazing a new trail for other developing countries to achieve modernization. It offers a new option for other countries and nations who want to speed up their development while preserving their independence; and it offers Chinese wisdom and a Chinese approach to solving the problems facing mankind.

This new era will be an era of building on past successes to further advance our cause, and of continuing in a new historical context to strive for the success of socialism with Chinese characteristics. It will be an era of securing a decisive victory in building a moderately prosperous society in all respects, and of moving on to all-out efforts to build a great modern socialist country. It will be an era for the Chinese people of all ethnic groups to work together and work hard to create a better life for themselves and ultimately achieve common prosperity for everyone. It will be an era for all of us, the sons and daughters of the Chinese nation, to strive with one heart to realize the Chinese Dream of national rejuvenation. It will be an era that sees China moving closer to center stage and making greater contributions to mankind.

Chinese socialism's entrance into a new era is, in the history of the People's Republic of China and the history of the

国发展史上、中华民族发展史上具有重大意义，在世界社会主义发展史上、人类社会发展史上也具有重大意义。

新时代要有新气象，更要有新作为。必须按照新时代的要求，完善发展战略和各项政策，推进和落实各项工作。

Chinese nation, of tremendous importance. In the history of international socialism and the history of human society, it is of tremendous importance.

With the arrival of the new era there are new expectations. It is essential to adjust our development strategy and policies in response to new realities.

习近平新时代中国特色社会主义思想

中共十八大以来，国内外形势变化和我国各项事业发展都给中国共产党提出了一个重大时代课题——这就是必须从理论和实践结合上系统回答新时代坚持和发展什么样的中国特色社会主义、怎样坚持和发展中国特色社会主义。围绕这个重大时代课题，中国共产党坚持以马克思列宁主义、毛泽东思想、邓小平理论、“三个代表”重要思想、科学发展观为指导，坚持解放思想、实事求是、与时俱进、求真务实，坚持辩证唯物主义和历史唯物主义，紧密结合新的时代条件和实践要求，以全

Xi Jinping Thought on Socialism with Chinese Characteristics for a New Era

Since the 18th CPC National Congress, changes both in and outside China and the progress made in all areas of China's endeavors have presented us with a major issue for a new era. The issue must be a systematic combination of theory and practice and must address what kind of socialism with Chinese characteristics the new era requires us to uphold and develop, and how we should go about doing it.

On this issue, our Party has been guided by Marxism-Leninism, Mao Zedong Thought, Deng Xiaoping Theory, the Theory of Three Represents, and the Scientific Outlook on Development. It has continued to free our minds, seek truth from facts, move with the times, and apply a realistic and pragmatic approach. On this issue, our Party has continued to uphold dialectical and historical materialism; has considered carefully the new conditions of the era and the new requirements of practice; and has adopted an entirely new perspective to have a deeper understanding of the laws that underlie governance by a Communist party, the development of socialism, and the evolution of human society.

新的视野深化对共产党执政规律、社会主义建设规律、人类社会发展规律的认识，通过艰辛理论探索，取得了重大理论创新成果，形成了习近平新时代中国特色社会主义思想。

习近平新时代中国特色社会主义思想，明确坚持和发展中国特色社会主义，总任务是实现社会主义现代化和中华民族伟大复兴，在全面建成小康社会的基础上，分两步走，在本世纪中叶建成富强民主文明和谐美丽的社会主义现代化强国；明确新时代我国社会主要矛盾是人民日益增长的美好生活需要和不平衡不充分的发展之间的矛盾，必须坚持以人民为中心的发展思想，不断促进人的全面发展、全体人民共同富裕；明确中国特色社会主义事业总体布局是“五位一体”、战略布局是“四个全面”，强调坚定道路自信、理论自

It has worked hard to undertake theoretical explorations, and has achieved major theoretical innovations, ultimately giving shape to Xi Jinping Thought on Socialism with Chinese Characteristics for a New Era.

Xi Jinping Thought on Socialism with Chinese Characteristics for a New Era makes the following things clear:

• It makes clear that the overarching task of upholding and developing socialism with Chinese characteristics is to realize socialist modernization and national rejuvenation, and that, on the basis of finishing the building of a moderately prosperous society in all respects, a two-step approach should be taken to build China into a great modern socialist country that is prosperous, strong, democratic, culturally advanced, harmonious, and beautiful by the middle of the century.

• It makes clear that the principal contradiction facing Chinese society in the new era is that between unbalanced and inadequate development and the people's ever-growing needs for a better life. We must therefore continue commitment to our people-centered philosophy of development and work to promote well-rounded human development and common prosperity for everyone.

• It makes clear that the overall plan for building socialism with Chinese characteristics is the Five-sphere Integrated Plan, and the overall strategy is the Four-pronged Comprehensive Strategy. It highlights the importance of fostering stronger confidence in the path, theory, system, and culture of

信、制度自信、文化自信；明确全面深化改革总目标是完善和发展中国特色社会主义制度、推进国家治理体系和治理能力现代化；明确全面推进依法治国总目标是建设中国特色社会主义法治体系、建设社会主义法治国家；明确党在新时代的强军目标是建设一支听党指挥、能打胜仗、作风优良的人民军队，把人民军队建设成为世界一流军队；明确中国特色大国外交要推动构建新型国际关系，推动构建人类命运共同体；明确中国特色社会主义最本质的特征是中国共产党领导，中国特色社会主义制度的最大优势是中国共产党领导，党是最高政治领导力量，提出新时代党的建设总要求，突出政治建设在党的建设中的重要地位。

习近平新时代中国特色社会主义思想，是对马克思列宁主义、毛泽东思想、邓小平理论、“三个代表”重要思想、科学

socialism with Chinese characteristics.

• It makes clear that the overall goal of continuing reform in every field is to improve and develop the system of socialism with Chinese characteristics and modernize China's system and capacity for governance.

• It makes clear that the overall goal of comprehensively advancing law-based governance is to establish a system of socialist rule of law with Chinese characteristics and build a country of socialist rule of law.

• It makes clear that the Party's goal of building a strong military in the new era is to build the people's armed forces into world-class forces that obey the Party's command, can fight and win, and maintain excellent conduct.

• It makes clear that major country diplomacy with Chinese characteristics aims to foster a new form of international relations and build a community with a shared future for humanity.

• It makes clear that the defining feature of socialism with Chinese characteristics is the leadership of the Communist Party of China; the greatest strength of the system of socialism with Chinese characteristics is the leadership of the Communist Party of China; the Party is the paramount force for political leadership. It sets forth the general requirements for Party building in the new era and underlines the importance of political development in Party building.

Xi Jinping Thought on Socialism with Chinese Characteristics for a New Era builds

发展观的继承和发展，是马克思主义中国化最新成果，是党和人民实践经验和集体智慧的结晶，是中国特色社会主义理论体系的重要组成部分，是全党全国人民为实现中华民族伟大复兴而奋斗的行动指南，必须长期坚持并不断发展。

on and further enriches Marxism-Leninism, Mao Zedong Thought, Deng Xiaoping Theory, the Theory of Three Represents, and the Scientific Outlook on Development. It represents the latest achievement in adapting Marxism to the Chinese context and encapsulates the practical experience and collective wisdom of our Party and the people. It is an important component of the theory of socialism with Chinese characteristics, and a guide to action for all Party members and all the Chinese people as we strive to achieve national rejuvenation. This Thought must be adhered to and steadily developed on a long-term basis.

新时代中国社会主要矛盾

中国特色社会主义进入新时代，社会主要矛盾已经转化为人民日益增长的美好生活需要和不平衡不充分的发展之间的矛盾。中国稳定解决了十几亿人的温饱问题，总体上实现小康，不久将全面建成小康社会，人民美好生活需求日益广泛，不仅对物质文化生活提出了更高要求，而且在民主、法治、公平、正义、安全、环境等方面的要求也日益增长。同时，中国社会生产力水平总体上显著提高，社会生产能力在很多方面进入世界前列，发展不平衡不充分的问题更加突出，这已经成为满足人民日益增长的美好生活需要的主要制约因素。

中国社会主要矛盾的变化是关系全局的历史性变化，对党和国家工作提出了许多新要求。特别是要在继续推动发展的基础上，着力解决好发展不平衡不充分问题，大力提升发展质量和效益，更好满足人民在经济、政治、文化、社会、生态等方面日益增长的需要，更好推动人的全面

Principal Contradiction Facing Chinese Society in a New Era

As socialism with Chinese characteristics has entered a new era, the principal contradiction facing Chinese society has evolved. What we now face is the contradiction between unbalanced and inadequate development and the people's ever-growing needs for a better life. China has seen the basic needs of over a billion people met, has basically made it possible for people to live decent lives, and will soon bring the building of a moderately prosperous society to a successful completion. The needs to be met for the people to live better lives are increasingly broad. Not only have their material and cultural needs grown; their demands for democracy, rule of law, fairness and justice, security, and a better environment are increasing. At the same time, China's overall productive forces have significantly improved and in many areas our production capacity leads the world. The more prominent problem is that our development is unbalanced and inadequate. This has become the main constraining factor in meeting the people's increasing needs for a better life.

We must recognize that the evolution of the principal contradiction facing Chinese society represents a historic shift that affects the whole landscape and that creates many new demands for the work of the Party and the

发展、社会全面进步。

中国社会主要矛盾的变化，没有改变中国共产党对中国社会主义所处历史阶段的判断，中国仍处于并将长期处于社会主义初级阶段的基本国情没有变，中国是世界最大发展中国家的国际地位没有变。中国共产党要牢牢把握社会主义初级阶段这个基本国情，牢牢立足社会主义初级阶段这个最大实际，牢牢坚持党的基本路线这个党和国家的生命线、人民的幸福线，领导和团结全国各族人民，以经济建设为中心，坚持四项基本原则，坚持改革开放，自力更生，艰苦创业，为把中国建设成为富强民主文明和谐美丽的社会主义现代化强国而奋斗。

country. Building on continued efforts to sustain development, we must devote great energy to addressing development's imbalances and inadequacies, and push hard to improve the quality and effect of development. With this, we will be better placed to meet the ever-growing economic, political, cultural, social, and ecological needs of our people, and to promote well-rounded human development and all-round social progress.

We must recognize that the evolution of the principal contradiction facing Chinese society does not change our assessment of the present stage of socialism in China. The basic dimension of the Chinese context – that our country is still and will long remain in the primary stage of socialism – has not changed. China's international status as the world's largest developing country has not changed. The whole Party must be completely clear about this fundamental dimension of our national context, and must base our work on this most important reality – the primary stage of socialism. We must remain fully committed to the Party's guideline as the source that keeps the Party and the country going and that brings happiness to the people. We must lead and unite the Chinese people of all ethnic groups in fulfilling the central task of economic development. We must uphold the Four Cardinal Principles, continue to reform and open up, be self-reliant, hardworking, and enterprising, and strive to build China into a great modern socialist country that is prosperous, strong, democratic, culturally advanced, harmonious, and beautiful.

中国梦

2012年11月29日，习近平在参观《复兴之路》展览时发表讲话，首次提出中国梦。实现中华民族伟大复兴，就是中华民族近代以来最伟大的梦想。这个梦想，凝聚了几代中国人的夙愿，体现了中华民族和中国人民的整体利益，是每一个中华儿女的共同期盼。到 2021 年中国共产党成立一百年时全面建成小康社会，到2035年基本实现现代化，到2049年中华人民共和国成立一百年时建成富强民主文明和谐美丽的社会主义现代化强国，实现中华民族伟大复兴的梦想。中国梦的基本内涵是实现国家富强、民族振兴、人民幸福。中国梦是国家的、民族的，也是每一个中国人的。中国梦归根到底是人民的梦。实现中国梦必须走中国道路，弘扬中国精神，凝聚中国力量。中国梦是和平、发展、合作、共赢的梦，不仅造福中国人民，也同

The Chinese Dream

Xi Jinping first explained his vision of the Chinese Dream on November 29, 2012, when visiting the exhibition "The Path to National Rejuvenation." National rejuvenation has been the greatest dream of the Chinese people since the beginning of modern times. It is a dream that spans generations, a dream that reflects our national interests, and a dream embraced by every Chinese.

We will strive to complete the building of a moderately prosperous society by 2021 when the CPC celebrates its 100th birthday, to basically achieve modernization, and to make China a modern socialist country that is prosperous, strong, democratic, culturally advanced, harmonious and beautiful by 2049, the 100th anniversary of the founding of the People's Republic. That is what our dream of national rejuvenation is all about.

In essence, the Chinese Dream is a commitment to bringing prosperity and happiness to our country, our nation and our people. It is a dream of our country, our nation, and our people. To make our dream come true, we must follow the Chinese path to development, elevate the Chinese spirit, and boost national cohesion.

The Chinese Dream is a dream of peace, development, cooperation and prosperity for all, benefiting not only the Chinese people but also the people of the rest of the

各国人民的美好梦想息息相通。实干才能梦想成真。中国梦不是镜中花、水中月，不是空洞的口号。人民对美好生活的向往就是中国共产党的奋斗目标。

world. Only by staying focused on achieving real results and making sustained and unwavering efforts can we bring our dream to fruition. The Chinese Dream is not a flower reflected in a mirror or a moon reflected in water. It is not an empty slogan. The goal of the CPC corresponds to the people's yearning for a better life and a brighter future.

决胜全面建成小康社会

改革开放之初，邓小平首先用“小康”来诠释中国式现代化，明确提出到20世纪末“在中国建立一个小康社会”的奋斗目标。在全党全国各族人民共同努力下，邓小平提出的目标在20世纪末如期实现，人民生活总体上达到小康水平。在这个基础上，党的十六大提出本世纪头20年全面建设惠及十几亿人口的更高水平的小康社会的目标；党的十七大提出了全面建设小康社会的新要求；党的十八大对全面建设小康社会目标进行了充实和完善，将“全面建设小康社会”调整为“全面建成小康社会”，顺应了人民的新要求；党的十九大报告指出，从现在到2020年，是全面建成小康社会决胜期。全面建成小康社会的奋斗目标，是党向人民、向历史作出的庄严承诺。这个宏伟目标，是“两个一百年”奋斗目标的第一个百年奋斗目标，是中华民族伟大复兴征程上的又一座重要里程碑。全面建成小康社会，“小康”讲的是发展水

Completing the Building of a Moderately Prosperous Society in All Respects

The vision of a moderately prosperous society was raised by Deng Xiaoping in the late 1970s and early 1980s, when the roadmap for China's economic and social development was being crafted. Thanks to the concerted efforts of the whole nation, the goal of a markedly improved life for the people had become a basic reality by the end of the 20th century.

Taking this into consideration, the CPC called for a continued push to build a moderately prosperous society in all respects in the report to the 16th National Congress (held in 2002). New and more ambitious elements were subsequently added to this expanded concept at the Party's 17th National Congress (held in 2007). On the basis of what had been achieved since the Party's previous two major gatherings, the CPC announced in the report to the 18th National Congress (held in 2012) the goal of completing the process of building a moderately prosperous society in all respects by the year 2020. The 19th National Congress of the CPC held in October 2017 described the period between now and 2020 as "decisive" in completing the process.

平，“全面”讲的是发展的平衡性、协调性、可持续性。全面建成小康社会，更重要、更难做到的是“全面”。全面建成小康社会，最艰巨最繁重的任务在农村、特别是在贫困地区，最根本最紧迫的任务还是进一步解放和发展社会生产力。

Fulfilling this goal is a solemn pledge the CPC has made to the Chinese people and the Chinese nation. It is the first of the Two Centennial Goals, and will be another milestone on China's journey toward national rejuvenation.

While "a moderately prosperous society" sets the goal for a higher level of social-economic development, "in all respects" requires balanced, sustainable, and properly coordinated development. The latter is the harder of the two challenges. The toughest and heaviest task is to help rural areas – poor areas in particular – and the most essential and urgent task is to further unlock and develop the nation's productive forces.

坚持党对一切工作的领导

中国共产党的领导，是历史的选择，人民的选择。中国共产党的领导是中国特色社会主义最本质的特征，是中国特色社会主义制度的最大优势。正因为如此，习近平总书记在党的十九大报告中，把“坚持党对一切工作的领导”作为新时代坚持和发展中国特色社会主义基本方略中的第一条。在实践中坚持党对一切工作的领导，必须增强政治意识、大局意识、核心意识、看齐意识，自觉维护党中央权威和集中统一领导，自觉在思想上政治上行动上同党中央保持高度一致，完善坚持党的领导的体制机制，坚持稳中求进工作总基

Ensuring CPC Leadership over All Work

China's modern history attests to the fact that the CPC's leadership role has been indispensable. It has been the choice of the people. CPC leadership is the defining feature of socialism with Chinese characteristics, which represents the greatest strength of our distinctly Chinese socialist system. Because of its paramount importance, it is included as the first of the basic policies for upholding and promoting socialism with Chinese characteristics for a new era in General Secretary Xi Jinping's report to the 19th CPC National Congress.

The Party exercises overall leadership over all areas of endeavor in every part of the country. We must strengthen our consciousness of the need to maintain political integrity, think in big picture terms, follow the leadership core, and keep in alignment. We must work harder to uphold the authority and centralized, unified leadership of the Central Committee, and closely follow the Central Committee in terms of our thinking, political orientation, and actions. We must improve the institutions and mechanisms for upholding Party leadership, remain committed to the underlying principle of pursuing progress while ensuring stability, and ensure coordinated implementation of

调，统筹推进“五位一体”总体布局，协调推进“四个全面”战略布局，提高党把方向、谋大局、定政策、促改革的能力和定力，确保党始终总揽全局、协调各方。

the Five-sphere Integrated Plan and the Four-pronged Comprehensive Strategy. We must strengthen the Party's ability and resolve to chart our course, craft overall plans, design policy, and promote reform; and we must ensure the Party always provides overall leadership and coordinates the efforts of all involved.

坚持以人民为中心

人民是历史的创造者，是决定党和国家前途命运的根本力量。党的十九大报告指出，必须坚持以人民为中心的发展思想，不断促进人的全面发展、全体人民共同富裕。人民立场是中国共产党的根本政治立场，是马克思主义政党区别于其他政党的显著标志。带领人民创造幸福生活，是党始终不渝的奋斗目标。以人民为中心的发展思想体现在经济社会发展各个环节。践行以人民为中心的发展思想，要坚持人民主体地位，顺应人民群众对美好生活的向往，不断实现好、维护好、发展好最广大人民的根本利益，做到发展为了人民、发展依靠人民、发展成果由人民共享。要通过深化改革、创新驱动，提高经济发展质量和效益，生产出更多更好的物质精神产品，不断满足人民日益增长的物质文化需要。要全面调动人的积极性、主动性、创造性，为各行业各方面的劳动者、企业家、创新人才、各级干部创造发挥作用的舞台和环境。要坚持社会主义基本经济制度和分配制度，调整收入分配格局，完善以税收、社会保障、转移支付等

A People-Centered Approach

The people are the creators of history. Their contribution determines the future of our Party and our country. In his report to the 19th CPC National Congress, Xi Jinping highlighted the importance of a people-centered approach to promoting human development and bringing prosperity to all. Our people-centered philosophy is key to the Party's political thinking. It is what distinguishes a Marxist party from other political parties, and is reflected in all our economic and social development initiatives, attesting to the centrality of the wellbeing of the people on the Party's agenda. Implementing such a philosophy calls for respect for the people's role in running the country and sensitivity to their yearning for a better life. It is our responsibility to always serve, defend and uphold the best interests of the people, and ensure that development is for the people, by the people and benefiting the people.

Further reform and innovation are critical to addressing quality and efficiency concerns in our development efforts, so as to produce more quality products to satisfy the people's growing material and cultural needs. It is essential to create an environment that encourages creativity and innovation, and helps individuals, including workers,

为主要手段的再分配调节机制，维护社会公平正义，解决好收入差距问题，使发展成果更多更公平惠及全体人民。以人民为中心的发展思想，体现了党全心全意为人民服务的根本宗旨，体现了人民是推动发展的根本力量的唯物史观，体现了逐步实现共同富裕的目标要求，彰显了党人民至上的价值取向。

entrepreneurs, innovators, and officials at all levels, realize their full potential. It is imperative to continue to strengthen and improve our basic socialist economic and distribution system, especially income redistribution mechanisms, including by rationalizing the taxation regime, strengthening social security, and increasing government transfer payments. These and other related measures aim to better ensure social equity and justice, narrow the existing income gap and more broadly and equitably share development gains.

Our people-centered development philosophy reflects the Party's overarching goal of serving the public good, and the principles of historical materialism that emphasizes the role of the people in turning the wheel of history. It is in line with our aspirations to bring prosperity to all and our value system that highlights the centrality of the people.

坚持全面深化改革

2013年11月召开的中共十八届三中全会审议通过了《中共中央关于全面深化改革若干重大问题的决定》，对全面深化改革作出总部署、总动员，勾画了到2020年全面深化改革的时间表、路线图。全面深化改革的总目标是：完善和发展中国特色社会主义制度，推进国家治理体系和治理能力现代化。全面深化改革不是推进一个领域改革，也不是推进几个领域改革，而是涉及经济、政治、文化、社会、生态文明、国防和军队以及对外开放等所有领域改革；它不是单靠某一个或某几个部门，而是需要协调各方；它不是阶段性任务，而是需要一代又一代人接力干下去。要坚决破除一切不合时宜的思想观念和体制机制弊端，突破利益固化的藩篱，吸收人类文明有益成果，构建系统完备、科学规范、运行有效的制度体系，充分发挥我国

In-Depth Reform in All Respects

The decision on issues concerning in-depth reform in all respects adopted by the 18th CPC Central Committee at its third plenary session presents an overall plan of action, a timetable and a roadmap for reform initiatives to be implemented by 2020. The overall goal of our all-round push for further reform is to improve and develop the socialist system with Chinese characteristics and to modernize China's governance system and capacity.

Reform will not be restricted to one or a few particular fields, but will involve a wide range of areas, including economic, political, cultural, social, and environmental policies, national defense, the military, and efforts to build a more open society. Success will not materialize with the efforts of a few particular departments, but will hinge on the concerted efforts of all actors. Our reform has no fixed timeframe; it is an on-going process that spans generations.

It entails resolve to break down all anachronistic barriers, whether ideological or institutional, and to overcome resistance from vested interests. It is crucial to draw upon useful experience of world civilization in our push to build a comprehensive, rational, rule-based, and effective framework that

社会主义制度优越性。推进全面深化改革的根本目的，就是要促进社会公平正义，让改革发展成果更多更公平惠及全体人民，让人民群众有更多获得感。

helps realize the full potential of our socialist system. The purpose of our reform is, in a word, to promote social equity and justice, and more broadly and equitably share development gains, so that benefits from reform are more tangibly felt.

坚持新发展理念

发展是解决中国一切问题的基础和关键，发展必须是科学发展，必须坚定不移贯彻创新、协调、绿色、开放、共享的发展理念。必须坚持和完善中国社会主义基本经济制度和分配制度，毫不动摇巩固和发展公有制经济，毫不动摇鼓励、支持、引导非公有制经济发展，使市场在资源配置中起决定性作用，更好发挥政府作用，推动新型工业化、信息化、城镇化、农业现代化同步发展，主动参与和推动经济全球化进程，发展更高层次的开放型经济，不断壮大中国经济实力和综合国力。

贯彻新发展理念的具体要求是：坚持质量第一、效益优先，以供给侧结构性改革为主线，推动经济发展质量变革、效率变革、动力变革，提高全要素生产率，着力加快建设实体经济、科技创新、现代金融、人力资源协同发展的产业体系，着力构建市场机制有效、微观主体有活力、宏观调控有度的经济体制，不断增强中国经济创新力和竞争力。坚持新发展理念要做好深化供给侧结构性改革、加快建设创新型国家、实施乡村振兴战略、实施区域协

New Concept for Development

Development is the underpinning of and the key to solving all our country's problems; our development must be sound development.

We must pursue with firmness of purpose the vision of innovative, coordinated, green, and open development that is for everyone.

We must uphold and improve China's basic socialist economic system and socialist distribution system. There must be no irresolution about working to consolidate and develop the public sector; and there must be no irresolution about working to encourage, support, and guide the development of the non-public sector. We must see that the market plays the decisive role in resource allocation, the government plays its role better, and new industrialization, IT application, urbanization, and agricultural modernization go hand in hand. We must actively participate in and promote economic globalization, develop an open economy of higher standards, and continue to increase China's economic power and composite strength.

We must put quality first and give priority to performance. We should pursue supply-side structural reform as our main task, and work hard for better quality, higher efficiency, and more robust drivers of economic growth

调发展战略、加快完善社会主义市场经济体制、推动形成全面开放新格局六个方面的工作。

through reform. We need to raise total factor productivity and accelerate the building of an industrial system that promotes coordinated development of the real economy with technological innovation, modern finance, and human resources. We should endeavor to develop an economy with more effective market mechanisms, dynamic micro-entities, and sound macro-regulation. This will steadily strengthen the innovation capacity and competitiveness of China's economy.

In addition to supply-side structural reforms, implementing the new concept for development entails efforts to make China a global leader in innovation, a rural revitalization drive, coordinated development at subnational levels, initiatives to improve the socialist market economy, and a strategy for greater openness.

坚持人民当家做主

在中国，国家的一切权力属于人民。正因为如此，“坚持人民当家做主”成为新时代坚持和发展中国特色社会主义基本方略之一。党的十九大报告强调，坚持党的领导、人民当家做主、依法治国有机统一是社会主义政治发展的必然要求。必须坚持中国特色社会主义政治发展道路，坚持和完善人民代表大会制度、中国共产党领导的多党合作和政治协商制度、民族区域自治制度、基层群众自治制度，巩固和发展最广泛的爱国统一战线，发展社会主义协商民主，健全民主制度，丰富民主形式，拓宽民主渠道，把保证人民当家做主落实到国家政治生活和社会生活之中。“坚持人民当家做主”彰显了中国社会主义民主是维护人民根本利益的最广泛、最真实、最管用的民主。发展社会主义民主

Running of the Country by the People

In China all power of the state belongs to the people. It is therefore only natural that respect for the running of the country by the people is included as one of the basic policies for upholding and promoting socialism with Chinese characteristics for a new era.

The report to the 19th CPC National Congress emphasizes the unity of the leadership by the CPC, the running of the country by the people and the rule of law as a natural element of socialist political advancement. Our resolve will not waver to continue on the path of socialist political development with Chinese characteristics, and to strengthen and improve people's congresses at all levels, multiparty cooperation and political consultation under the leadership of the CPC, regional ethnic autonomy, and community-level self-governance. Our objectives are, among others, to strengthen and develop a broadest possible patriotic united front, improve socialist consultative democracy and our democratic institutions, diversify our forms of democracy, and establish more democratic channels of interaction between the government and the public, so as to ensure that respect for the people's role is incorporated in all aspects of political and social life.

Respect for the people's role in the

政治，就是要体现人民意志、保障人民权益、激发人民创造活力，用制度体系保证人民当家做主。

running of the country ensures the broadest reach, the most practical nature and the greatest effectiveness of China's socialist democracy in safeguarding the fundamental interests of the people. The very purpose of developing socialist democracy is to give full expression to the will of the people, protect their rights and interests, encourage creativity and innovation, and provide an institutional framework that ensures the role of the people.

坚持全面依法治国

2014年10月召开的中共十八届四中全会作出了“全面推进依法治国”的部署。全面依法治国是中国特色社会主义的本质要求和重要保障。当前，中国面对的改革发展稳定任务之重前所未有，矛盾风险挑战之多前所未有，比以往任何时候都更加需要运用法治思维和法治方式开展工作、解决问题，更好发挥法治的引领和规范作用。全面依法治国的总目标是：建设中国特色社会主义法治体系，建设社会主义法治国家。为实现这一目标，需要形成完备的法律规范体系、高效的法治实施体系、严密的法治监督体系、有力的法治保障体系，以及完善的党内法规体系。在全面推进依法治国进程中，要坚持依法治国、依法执政、依法行政共同推进，坚持法治国家、法治政府、法治社会一体建设，实现科学立法、严格执法、公正司法、全民守法。全面依法治国，必须紧紧围绕保障和促进社会公平正义来进行，努力让人民群众在每一个司法案件中都能感受到公平正义。全面依法治国是一个系统工程，是国家治理领域一场广泛而深刻的革命。必须

Advancing Law-Based Governance

A comprehensive agenda for promoting the rule of law was launched by the 18th CPC Central Committee at its fourth plenary session in October 2014. Promoting the rule of law is indispensable to promoting socialism with Chinese characteristics.

In view of the fact that China is currently faced with unprecedented challenges in moving forward with further reform, and ensuring development and stability, a rule-of-law culture has become more important than ever before in guiding our work and our thinking in addressing these challenges.

The broad goal of a comprehensive agenda for promoting the rule of law is to build a socialist legal system with Chinese characteristics as part of our efforts to build a socialist country where the rule of law is respected. To this end, it is necessary to have in place a complete set of legal norms, efficient enforcement measures, rigorous oversight mechanisms, effective legal protections, and a complete body of internal Party regulations.

The comprehensive process of promoting the rule of law should focus on ensuring that our Constitution and laws are fully complied with in national governance and in the exercise of political and executive

把党的领导贯彻落实到依法治国全过程和各方面，坚定不移走中国特色社会主义法治道路。

power. Coordinated efforts should be made to strengthen our legal system and legal awareness throughout the country, at all levels of the government, and in all sectors of society, so as to ensure the rationality of our legislative process, strict enforcement of and universal adherence to all laws, and impartial administration of justice.

It is also essential in this regard to ensure and foster social equity and justice so that people feel that justice is done in all cases. Promoting the rule of law is a system engineering project, a revolution in China's governance with wide-ranging ramifications.

Leadership by the Party is indispensable in all aspects throughout the process of promoting the rule of law. Our determination to promote socialist rule of law with Chinese characteristics remains unshaken.

坚持社会主义核心价值体系

文化自信是一个国家、一个民族发展中更基本、更深沉、更持久的力量。2006年10月召开的中共十六届六中全会提出建设社会主义核心价值体系，并指出社会主义核心价值体系包括四个方面的基本内容：马克思主义指导思想、中国特色社会主义共同理想、以爱国主义为核心的民族精神和以改革创新为核心的时代精神、社会主义荣辱观。

Promoting the Core Values of Socialism

Cultural confidence is what sustains the development of a country or a nation in a most fundamental and profound sense. A plan to promote the core values of socialism was introduced by the 16th CPC Central Committee at its sixth plenary session in October 2006. Core values of socialism encompass the guiding principles of Marxism, the ideals of socialism with Chinese characteristics, the national spirit of patriotism, a commitment to reform and innovation, and a socialist honor code.

坚持在发展中保障和改善民生

增进民生福祉是发展的根本目的。必须多谋民生之利、多解民生之忧，在发展中补齐民生短板、促进社会公平正义，在幼有所育、学有所教、劳有所得、病有所医、老有所养、住有所居、弱有所扶上不断取得新进展，深入开展脱贫攻坚，保证全体人民在共建共享发展中有更多获得感，不断促进人的全面发展、全体人民共同富裕。建设平安中国，加强和创新社会治理，维护社会和谐稳定，确保国家长治久安、人民安居乐业。

在发展中保障和改善民生的具体要求是：抓住人民最关心最直接最现实的利益问题，既尽力而为，又量力而行，一件事情接着一件事情办，一年接着一年干。坚持人人尽责、人人享有，坚守底线、突出重点、完善制度、引导预期，完善公共服务体系，保障群众基本生活，不断满足人民日益增长的美好生活需要，不断促进社会公平正义，形成有效的社会治理、良好的社会秩序，使人民获得感、幸福感、安全感更加充实、更有保障、更可持续。坚

Improving the Wellbeing of the People

Improving the wellbeing of the people is the fundamental goal of development. It should indeed be the focus of all development efforts. We must be proactive in addressing the concerns of the people and areas of weakness, and promoting social fairness and justice. Efforts must continue to expand access to childcare, education, employment, medical services, elderly care, housing, and social assistance. Our poverty alleviation campaign must be intensified, to ensure that the impact of our joint development efforts is more broadly felt as everyone contributes to and gains from these efforts. It is critical in this respect to promote human development and bring prosperity to all. We will continue to implement the Peaceful China initiative, strengthen and improve social governance in an innovative manner, and promote social harmony and stability, so as to ensure our country's enduring peace and prosperity.

To improve the wellbeing of the people through development efforts, we must focus on the most pressing, most immediate issues that concern the people. We will do everything within the limits of available resources to tackle these issues. A step-by-step approach will be pursued in this endeavor that will go on for years. Improving the wellbeing of the

持在发展中保障和改善民生要做好优先发展教育事业、提高就业质量和人民收入水平、加强社会保障体系建设、坚决打赢脱贫攻坚战、实施健康中国战略、打造共建共治共享的社会治理格局、有效维护国家安全七个方面的工作。

people concerns and benefits everyone and requires contribution from everyone. The bottom line is to meet the basic needs of the people. It is essential to identify priority areas, improve institutional arrangements, and properly manage public expectations. Public services must be improved, not only to ensure that the people's basic needs are met, but also to satisfy their ever-growing needs for a better life. We will continue to promote social fairness and justice through effective social governance to build a well-ordered society, where individuals are able to realize their full potential, and can enjoy happiness and security.

Specific measures in this regard include improving education, creating more better jobs and raising income, strengthening the social security system, eliminating poverty, implementing the Healthy China initiative, building a participatory social governance structure that benefits all, and safeguarding national security.

坚持人与自然和谐共生

建设生态文明是中华民族永续发展的千年大计。必须树立和践行绿水青山就是金山银山的理念，坚持节约资源和保护环境的基本国策，像对待生命一样对待生态环境，统筹山水林田湖草系统治理，实行最严格的生态环境保护制度，形成绿色发展方式和生活方式，坚定走生产发展、生活富裕、生态良好的文明发展道路，建设美丽中国，为人民创造良好生产生活环境，为全球生态安全作出贡献。

坚持人与自然和谐共生的具体要求是：既要创造更多物质财富和精神财富以满足人民日益增长的美好生活需要，也要提供更多优质生态产品以满足人民日益增长的优美生态环境需要。必须坚持节约优先、保护优先、自然恢复为主的方针，形成节约资源和保护环境的空间格局、产业结构、生产方式、生活方式，还自然以宁静、和谐、美丽。坚持人与自然和谐共生

Achieving Harmony Between Man and Nature

Preserving and protecting our natural environment is vital to the survival of our nation. It is important to understand that "green mountains are gold mountains," and this understanding must be put into practice. As part of our basic national policy, we will step up efforts to conserve resources and protect the environment in the same manner as we protect our own lives. A holistic approach is critical to conservation programs aimed at protecting our mountains, rivers, forests, farmlands, lakes, and grasslands. Most stringent measures are necessary for fragile ecosystems. We will be unwavering in our pursuit of green development to ensure that economic growth and prosperity will not come at the expense of the environment. Environmental considerations will always inform our development efforts. We will continue to implement the Beautiful China initiative and create a better working and living environment for our people. In so doing, we are also contributing to global ecological security.

To achieve harmony between man and nature, we need to ensure the provision of more quality ecological goods and create a beautiful environment that our people crave, in addition to creating more material and cultural

要做好推进绿色发展、着力解决突出环境问题、加大生态系统保护力度、改革生态环境监管体制四个方面的工作。

wealth to meet their ever-increasing needs for a better life. Specific initiatives include resource conservation, and special protection and conservation measures aimed at helping nature restore itself. An integrated approach is needed to align resource conservation and environmental protection measures with efforts to readjust the economic structure and change the existing production and consumption patterns, so as to restore nature's serenity, harmony, and beauty.

To this end, we will continue to promote green development, tackle thorny environmental issues, strengthen protection for ecosystems, and reform environmental regulatory mechanisms.

坚持总体国家安全观

统筹发展和安全，增强忧患意识，做到居安思危，是中国共产党治国理政的一个重大原则。2014年4月，习近平在主持召开中央国家安全委员会第一次会议时强调，坚持总体国家安全观，以人民安全为宗旨，以政治安全为根本，以经济安全为基础，以军事、文化、社会安全为保障，以促进国际安全为依托，走出一条中国特色国家安全道路。总体国家安全观要求：既重视外部安全，又重视内部安全，对内求发展、求变革、求稳定、建设平安中国，对外求和平、求合作、求共赢、建设和谐世界；既重视国土安全，又重视国民安全，坚持以民为本、以人为本，坚持国家安全一切为了人民、一切依靠人民，真正夯实国家安全的群众基础；既重视传统安全，又重视非传统安全，构建集政治安全、国土安全、军事安全、经济安全、文化安全、社会安全、科技安全、信息安全、生态安全、资源安全、核安全等于一体的国家安全体系；既重视发展问题，又重视安全问题，发展是安全的基础，安全

A Holistic Approach to National Security

We should ensure both development and security and be ever ready to protect against potential dangers in time of peace. This is a major principle underlying the Party's governance.

While presiding over the first meeting of the National Security Commission of the CPC Central Committee in April 2014, Xi Jinping emphasized the need to take a holistic view of national security. Through such an approach, a full spectrum of security issues are assessed, ranging from people's security, which is the ultimate concern, political security, which is of overarching importance, and economic security, which underpins all other considerations, to military, cultural and social perspectives, which reinforce efforts in other areas, and the promotion of international security, which provides support for measures taken in a national context. Along this line of thinking we are setting out to build a national security system with Chinese characteristics.

Such a holistic approach requires a focus on both internal and external security. Internally, it is essential to promote development, continue reform, maintain stability, and create a safe environment. Externally, we should promote international peace, seek cooperation and mutual benefit, and strive to

是发展的条件；既重视自身安全，又重视共同安全，打造命运共同体，推动各方朝着互利互惠、共同安全的目标相向而行。要完善国家安全制度体系，加强国家安全能力建设，坚决维护国家主权、安全、发展利益。

bring harmony to the world. Homeland security and the security of our citizens are both of paramount importance. All initiatives taken in this respect will be people-centered, and implemented for the people, on the basis of the people's needs, and with the support of the people. Security issues, both traditional and non-traditional, will be taken into account. The national security system we envisage will integrate not only political security and homeland security, but also security-related military, economic, cultural, and social concerns, science and technology, information, ecological, resource, and nuclear security. Development issues will be considered in tandem with security issues. Development provides a basis for security, whereas security constitutes a necessary condition for development. Our national security must also be viewed in the context of international security. For the sake of our global community with a shared future, we should all work toward our goal of satisfying the world's security needs in a way that is beneficial to all. We will continue to improve our national security system, strengthen our national security capacity, and defend our sovereignty, security and national interest as it concerns our development needs.

坚持党对人民军队的绝对领导

坚持党对军队的绝对领导是人民军队建军的根本原则。建设一支听党指挥、能打胜仗、作风优良的人民军队，是实现“两个一百年”奋斗目标、实现中华民族伟大复兴的战略支撑。建军90年来，人民军队从小到大、由弱到强、从胜利走向胜利，最根本的是靠党的坚强领导，这是人民军队的命脉所在。坚持党对军队的绝对领导是强军兴军的根本保证。必须全面贯彻党领导人民军队的一系列根本原则和制度，确立新时代党的强军思想在国防和军队建设中的指导地位，坚持政治建军、改革强军、科技兴军、依法治军，更加注重聚焦实战，更加注重创新驱动，更加注重体系

The Party's Firm Leadership of the People's Armed Forces

The CPC's firm leadership of the people's armed forces is a fundamental principle of China's military policy. Building a well-disciplined military under the Party's command, able to fight and win major wars, is of strategic importance to achieving the Two Centennial Goals and bringing about national rejuvenation. Over the past 90 years since its founding, our military has emerged from a small guerrilla army into a powerful modern fighting force after scoring one victory after another. It owes this transformation to the Party's strong leadership role, which has become the lifeline of the people's armed forces.

Leadership by the Party is therefore key to any effort to build a strong military. This and other related principles must be implemented fully. The Party's military thinking should guide all decision-making processes when it comes to defense issues and the military. Measures in this regard include raising political awareness, implementing further reform, upgrading technology, and promoting law-based governance. More emphasis will be placed on improving combat capabilities. It is important to encourage innovation, improve institutional arrangements, enhance the efficiency of

建设，更加注重集约高效，更加注重军民融合，实现党在新时代的强军目标。

coordination between different services, and strengthen military-civilian integration, so as to realize the Party's goal of building a strong military for a new era.

坚持“一国两制”和推进祖国统一

“一国两制”的基本内容是：在一个中国的前提下，国家的主体坚持社会主义制度；香港、澳门、台湾是中华人民共和国不可分离的部分，它们作为特别行政区保持原有的资本主义制度长期不变。在国际上代表中国的，只能是中华人民共和国。“一国两制”是中国的一个伟大创举，是中华民族为世界和平与发展作出的新贡献。香港、澳门回归祖国以来，“一国两制”实践取得举世公认的成功。事实证明，“一国两制”是解决历史遗留的香港、澳门问题的最佳方案，也是香港、澳门回归后保持长期繁荣稳定的最佳制度。继续推进“一国两制”事业，是中央政府、特别行政区政府和包括港澳同胞在内的全国各族人民的共同使命。中央贯彻“一国两制”方针坚持两点，一是坚定不移，不会变、不动摇；二是全面准确，确保“一国两制”在港澳的实践不走样、不变形，始终沿着正确方向前进。当然，作为一项前无古人的

"One Country, Two Systems" and National Reunification

Under the "One Country, Two Systems" framework, there is but one China, and Hong Kong, Macao and Taiwan are inseparable parts of the People's Republic of China, but they will retain their existing capitalist system for a prolonged period of time as special administrative regions, while the rest of China implements a socialist system. Internationally, however, the PRC alone represents China. The "One Country, Two Systems" formula is a remarkable Chinese invention and an important contribution that China has made to world peace and development. It has been a widely acknowledged success since the return of Hong Kong and Macao to China, proved to be the best possible solution to the issues of Hong Kong and Macao – issues left over from history, and credited for sustained prosperity and stability there.

It is a shared mission of the central government, the administrations of the two special administrative regions, and the Chinese people including the people of Hong Kong and Macao to continue implementing the "One Country, Two Systems" model. The central government follows two principles in this regard. First, it remains committed to this model and will never change or waver on its

开创性事业，“一国两制”的实践不会一帆风顺，需要在实践中不断探索。

position. Second, the model must be implemented exactly as it was originally agreed upon without any distortion. Unprecedented in history, this groundbreaking endeavor will not be smooth sailing, and there will be much to learn along the way.

坚持推动构建人类命运共同体

党的十九大报告提出，各国人民同心协力，构建人类命运共同体，建设持久和平、普遍安全、共同繁荣、开放包容、清洁美丽的世界。要相互尊重、平等协商，坚决摒弃冷战思维和强权政治，走对话而不对抗、结伴而不结盟的国与国交往新路。要坚持以对话解决争端、以协商化解分歧，统筹应对传统和非传统安全威胁，反对一切形式的恐怖主义。要同舟共济，促进贸易和投资自由化便利化，推动经济全球化朝着更加开放、包容、普惠、平衡、共赢的方向发展。要尊重世界文明多样性，以文明交流超越文明隔阂、文明互鉴超越文明冲突、文明共存超越文明优

Building a Community with a Shared Future for Humanity

In his report to the 19th CPC National Congress, Xi Jinping called on the people of all countries to work together to build a community with a shared future for humanity, to build an open, inclusive, clean, and beautiful world that enjoys lasting peace, universal security, and common prosperity. We should respect each other, discuss issues as equals, resolutely reject the Cold War mentality and power politics, and take a new approach to developing state-to-state relations with communication, not confrontation, and with partnership, not alliance. We should commit ourselves to settling disputes through dialog and resolving differences through discussion, coordinate responses to traditional and non-traditional threats, and oppose terrorism in all its forms.

We should stick together through thick and thin, promote trade and investment liberalization and facilitation, and make economic globalization more open, inclusive, and balanced so that its benefits are shared by all. We should respect the diversity of civilizations. In handling relations among civilizations, let us replace estrangement with exchange, clashes with mutual learning, and superiority with coexistence. We should be

越。要坚持环境友好，合作应对气候变化，保护好人类赖以生存的地球家园。

good friends to the environment, cooperate to tackle climate change, and protect our planet for the sake of human survival.

坚持全面从严治党

2014年12月，习近平总书记在江苏考察时，提出了“全面从严治党”的新要求，把管党治党提到前所未有的新高度。办好中国的事情，关键在党，关键在党要管党、从严治党。勇于自我革命，从严管党治党，是中国共产党最鲜明的品格。全面从严治党，核心是加强党的领导，基础在全面，关键在严，要害在治。“全面”就是管全党、治全党，面向八千多万党员、四百多万个党组织，覆盖党的建设各个领域、各个方面、各个部门，重点是抓住“关键少数”。“从严”就是真管真严、敢管敢严、长管长严。“治党”就是从党中央到省市县党委，从中央部委、国家机关部门党组（党委）到基层党支部，都要肩负起主体责任，党委书记要把抓好党建当作分内之事、必须担当的职责；各级纪委要担负起监督责任，勇于执纪问责。要着重从思想从严、管党从严、执纪从严、治吏从严、作风从严、反腐从严六个方面入手，把全面从严治党落实到思想建设、组织建设、作风建设、反腐倡廉建设、制度建设等各个方面。从严治党最根本的就是使全

Enforcing Strict Party Self-Governance

During an inspection tour in Jiangsu Province in December 2014, General Secretary Xi Jinping emphasized the need to conduct strict Party self-governance, bringing it to an unprecedented level of importance. The key to national governance is a well-functioning and well-disciplined Party.

To have the courage to carry out self-reform and conduct strict self-governance: This is the most distinctive part of the CPC's character.

Central to the campaign to enforce strict Party discipline is strong Party leadership. The campaign must be wide-ranging, reaching its more than 80 million members and its more than four million subsidiary organizations, covering all aspects and all branches of the Party structure, with a special focus on oversight over the "key few." It must be vigorous, accompanied by forceful, bold and sustained measures. It must be effective to ensure greater accountability within the Party, from the Central Committee to Party committees at the provincial, municipal and county levels, and from central Party organizations and groups in national government agencies to branches at grassroots levels. Party secretaries are required to shoulder Party development tasks as an integral part of

党各级组织和全体党员、干部按照党内政治生活准则和党的各项规定办事。全面从严治党，要坚持思想建党和制度治党紧密结合，全方位扎紧制度笼子，更多用制度治党、管权、治吏。把全面从严治党纳入“四个全面”战略布局，是新的历史条件下我们党应对世情国情党情变化的必然选择。全面从严治党永远在路上。

their duty. Party disciplinary commissions at all levels are tasked with conducting oversight and enforcing accountability.

Enforcing strict Party discipline should be approached from six angles: political awareness, Party development measures, accountability enforcement, oversight, enforcement of ethical standards, and anti-corruption mechanisms. Also important is institution building. Above all, Party organizations at all levels and all members and officials must abide by the Party's guidelines on internal political conduct and its various rules. Political awareness initiatives and institution building should go hand in hand. Stronger institutional constraints must be in place at all levels, and so must more institutional oversight over the Party, over any exercise of authority, and over officials. The Party incorporates the need to enforce strict Party discipline as one of the four key components in its Four-pronged Comprehensive Strategy in response to changes both within itself and in the world under the new historical conditions. This is a journey to which there is no end.

坚持稳中求进工作总基调

十八大以来，习近平在国内外多个场合谈及“稳中求进工作总基调”，近几年的中央经济工作会议也都将稳中求进作为第二年工作的总基调。2016年12月，中央经济工作会议强调稳中求进工作总基调是治国理政的重要原则，也是做好经济工作的方法论。坚持稳中求进工作总基调，“稳”的重点要放在稳住经济运行上，确保增长、就业、物价不出现大的波动，确保金融不出现区域性系统性风险。“稳”是主基调，稳是大局，在“稳”的前提下要在关键领域有所进取，在把握好度的前提下奋发有为。“进”的重点要放在调整经济结构和深化改革开放上，确保转变经济发展方式和创新驱动发展取得新成效。“稳”和“进”要相互促进，经济社会平稳，才能为调整经济结构和深化改革开放创造稳定宏

Making Progress While Maintaining Stability as the Guideline

On many occasions since the 18th CPC National Congress, at home and abroad, Xi Jinping has referred to making progress while maintaining stability as the guideline for the work of the government. At each session of the Central Economic Work Conference in the last few years, this has been set as the guideline for work to be carried out in the following year. At one such meeting in December 2016, this guideline was again emphasized as an important principle for the country's governance and an effective approach to handling the economy.

As we pursue stability, we will focus on achieving steady economic performance, without sharp fluctuations in growth, employment, or prices, and without any regional or systemic risks in the financial sector. Stability is the principle that is important to our long-term goals. While maintaining stability, we need to make progress at the same time in key areas and to the extent that is possible.

When we make progress, we will focus on economic structural adjustment and further reform, to make progress in transforming our growth model and in innovation-driven development.

Stability and progress must happen

观环境；调整经济结构和深化改革开放取得实质性进展，才能为经济社会平稳运行创造良好预期。

at the same time in economy and society, in order to create an environment for structural transformation and further reform. And substantive progress must be made in transformation and reform before we can expect positive and stable economic and social development.

统筹推进“五位一体”总体布局

2012年11月8日，中共第十八次全国代表大会提出经济建设、政治建设、文化建设、社会建设、生态文明建设五位一体的建设中国特色社会主义总体布局。在坚持以经济建设为中心的同时，全面推进经济建设、政治建设、文化建设、社会建设、生态文明建设，促进现代化建设各个环节、各个方面协调发展。“五位一体”和“四个全面”相互促进、统筹联动，在推动经济发展的基础上，建设社会主义市场经济、民主政治、先进文化、生态文明、和谐社会，协同推进人民富裕、国家强盛、中国美丽。“五位一体”总体布局的提出，体现了中国共产党对协调发展认识的不断深化，对中国特色社会主义规律认识的不断深化。

The Five-Sphere Integrated Plan

The Five-sphere Integrated Plan – the development of socialism with Chinese characteristics encompassing economic, political, cultural, social and ecological development – was proposed on November 8, 2012 at the 18th National Congress of the CPC. While economic development continues to be the central pillar, economic, political, cultural, social and ecological development are to be promoted on all fronts, modernization is to be fostered in all areas, and all elements are to be developed in a coordinated manner. The Five-sphere Integrated Plan and the Four-pronged Comprehensive Strategy support each other and interact in a planned manner. Proceeding from economic growth, they help develop a socialist market economy, democratic governance, advanced culture, ecological progress, and a harmonious society. Together, they help make the people more prosperous, the country stronger, and China more beautiful. The enunciation of the Five-sphere Integrated Plan illustrates how the CPC continues to extend its understanding of coordinated development and of the framework of socialism with Chinese characteristics.

协调推进“四个全面”战略布局

2014年12月，习近平在江苏省调研时，明确提出了“四个全面”战略布局，即全面建成小康社会、全面深化改革、全面依法治国、全面从严治党。“四个全面”战略布局是从中国发展现实需要中得出来的，是从人民群众的热切期待中得出来的，是为推动解决中国面临的突出矛盾和问题提出来的。“四个全面”战略布局，相互之间密切联系、有机统一，具有紧密的内在逻辑，是一个整体战略部署的有序展开，共同支撑起中国特色社会主义事业全局。全面建成小康社会是重大战略目标，在“四个全面”战略布局中居于引领地位。全面深化改革、全面依法治国、全面从严治党是三大战略举措，为如期全面建成小康社会提供重要保障。“四个全面”战略布

The Four-Pronged Comprehensive Strategy

During an inspection tour in Fujian Province in November 2014, Xi Jinping spoke explicitly about the Three-pronged Comprehensive Strategy, which consists of completing the building of a society which is moderately prosperous in all respects, comprehensively expanding in-depth reform, and comprehensively promoting law-based governance. In the following month when making an inspection tour in Jiangsu Province, he added "comprehensively enforcing strict Party self-governance" to form the Four-pronged Comprehensive Strategy. This Four-pronged Comprehensive Strategy emerged from China's actual developmental needs and from the expectations of the people, and was formulated to help solve the most pressing problems and issues currently facing the country.

The four prongs are closely interconnected, holistically integrated and tightly linked by their internal logic. They are organized in an orderly manner by an overarching strategic plan, and together they support the overall development of Chinese socialism. Completing the building of a society which is moderately prosperous in all respects is the foremost element of the Four-pronged Comprehensive Strategy. The other three

局，确立了新的历史条件下党和国家各项工作的战略目标和战略举措，是党在新形势下治国理政的总方略，是事关党和国家长远发展的总战略，为实现“两个一百年”奋斗目标、实现中华民族伟大复兴的中国梦提供了重要保障。

measures – comprehensively expanding in-depth reform, comprehensively promoting law-based governance, and comprehensively enforcing strict Party self-governance – provide important guarantees for completing the building of a moderately prosperous society in all respects as planned.

The Four-pronged Comprehensive Strategy spells out strategic goals and measures for the Party and the country under the new historical circumstances, and is the Party's master plan for the nation's governance for a new era. It is an overall strategy for the long-term development of the Party and the country, and an important guarantee of the Chinese Dream of great national rejuvenation.

“十三五”规划

“十三五”规划是《中华人民共和国国民经济和社会发展第十三个五年规划纲要》的简称，起止时间为2016年—2020年，于2016年3月正式对外发布。“十三五”规划阐明了“十三五”期间的国家战略意图，明确了经济社会发展宏伟目标、主要任务和重大举措，是市场主体的行为导向，是政府履行职责的重要依据，是全国各族人民的共同愿景。“十三五”规划提出了“到2020年全面建成小康社会”的奋斗目标，并首次提出“创新、协调、绿色、开放、共享”五大发展理念。按照全面建成小康社会新的目标要求，“十三五”规划确定了经济社会发展五个方面的主要目标：经济保持中高速增长、人民生活水平和质量普遍提高、国民素质和社会文明程度显著提高、生态环境质量总体改善、各方面制度更加成熟更加定型。

The 13th Five-Year Plan

"The 13th Five-year Plan," officially published in March 2016, is the short form for the 13th Five-year Plan of the People's Republic of China on National Economic and Social Development. The Plan has set the strategic goals for national development from 2016 to 2020, with specific objectives, tasks and measures outlined for implementation. It serves as a guide for market entities and as an important frame of reference by which the government performs its functions. In sum, it embodies the aspirations of the Chinese people for a better life as it sets the goal to build a moderately prosperous society in all respects by the year 2020.

It presented for the first time the Five Concepts for Development: innovative, coordinated, green, open, and inclusive. In order to achieve the goal of building a moderately prosperous society, the Plan identifies targets for economic and social development in five areas:

• steady economic growth at medium-high speed;

• extensive improvement of living standards;

• improvement of the cultural level of the population and a rise in ethical standards;

• overall enhancement of the quality of the environment; and

• well-established systems and structures in different areas.

全面建设社会主义现代化强国

从中共十九大到中共二十大，是中国“两个一百年”奋斗目标的历史交汇期。中共十九大报告提出，既要全面建成小康社会、实现第一个百年奋斗目标，又要乘势而上开启全面建设社会主义现代化国家新征程，向第二个百年奋斗目标进军。中共十九大综合分析国际国内形势和中国发展条件，提出从2020年到本世纪中叶可以分两个阶段来安排。

第一个阶段，从2020年到2035年，在全面建成小康社会的基础上，再奋斗十五年，基本实现社会主义现代化。到那时，中国经济实力、科技实力将大幅跃升，跻身创新型国家前列；人民平等参与、平等发展权利得到充分保障，法治国家、法治政府、法治社会基本建成，各

Building a Modern Socialist China in All Respects

The period between the 19th and the 20th CPC National Congress is the period in which the timeframes of the Two Centennial Goals converge. In this period, not only must we finish building a moderately prosperous society in all respects and achieve the first centennial goal; we must also build on this achievement to embark on a new journey toward the second centennial goal of fully building a modern socialist country. Based on a comprehensive analysis of the international and domestic environments and the conditions for China's development, we have drawn up a two-stage development plan for the period from 2020 to the middle of this century.

In the first stage from 2020 to 2035, we will build on the foundation created by the moderately prosperous society with a further 15 years of hard work to see that socialist modernization is basically realized. The vision is that by the end of this stage, the following goals will have been met:

• China's economic and technological strength has increased significantly. China has become a global leader in innovation.

• The rights of the people to participate and to develop as equals are adequately protected. The rule of law for the country, the

方面制度更加完善，国家治理体系和治理能力现代化基本实现；社会文明程度达到新的高度，国家文化软实力显著增强，中华文化影响更加广泛深入；人民生活更为宽裕，中等收入群体比例明显提高，城乡区域发展差距和居民生活水平差距显著缩小，基本公共服务均等化基本实现，全体人民共同富裕迈出坚实步伐；现代社会治理格局基本形成，社会充满活力又和谐有序；生态环境根本好转，美丽中国目标基本实现。

第二个阶段，从2035年到本世纪中叶，在基本实现现代化的基础上，再奋斗十五年，把中国建成富强民主文明和谐美丽的社会主义现代化强国。到那时，中国物质文明、政治文明、精神文明、社会文明、生态文明将全面提升，实现国家治理体系和治理能力现代化，成为综合国力和国际影响力领先的国家，全体人民共同富裕基本实现，中国人民将享有更加幸福安康的生活，中华民族将以更加昂扬的姿态

government, and society is basically in place. Institutions in all fields are further improved; the modernization of China's system and capacity for governance is basically achieved.

• Social etiquette and civility are significantly enhanced. China's cultural soft power has grown much stronger; Chinese culture has greater appeal.

• People are leading more comfortable lives, and the size of the middle-income group has grown considerably. Disparities in urban-rural development, in development between regions, and in living standards are significantly reduced; equitable access to basic public services is basically ensured; and solid progress has been made toward prosperity for everyone.

• A modern social governance system has taken shape, and society is full of vitality, harmonious, and orderly.

• There is a fundamental improvement in the environment; the goal of building a Beautiful China is basically attained.

In the second stage from 2035 to the middle of the 21st century, we will, building on having basically achieved modernization, work hard for a further 15 years and develop China into a great modern socialist country that is prosperous, strong, democratic, culturally advanced, harmonious, and beautiful. By the end of this stage, the following goals will have been met:

• New heights are reached in every dimension of material, political, cultural and ethical, social, and ecological advancement.

屹立于世界民族之林。

从全面建成小康社会到基本实现现代化，再到全面建成社会主义现代化强国，是新时代中国特色社会主义发展的战略安排。

• Modernization of China's system and capacity for governance is achieved.

• China has become a global leader in terms of composite national strength and international influence.

• Common prosperity for everyone is basically achieved.

• The Chinese people enjoy happier, safer, and healthier lives.

• The Chinese nation will become a proud and active member of the community of nations.

This is our strategic vision for developing socialism with Chinese characteristics in a new era: Finish building a moderately prosperous society in all respects, move on to basically realizing modernization, and then turn to making China a great modern socialist country in every dimension.

新时代中国共产党的历史使命

The New Era: The Historic Mission of the Communist Party of China

中国共产党人的初心和使命

中国共产党人的初心和使命，就是为中国人民谋幸福，为中华民族谋复兴。这个初心和使命是激励中国共产党人不断前进的根本动力。

不忘初心，方得始终。九十多年来，为了实现中华民族伟大复兴的历史使命，无论是弱小还是强大，无论是顺境还是逆境，中国共产党都初心不改、矢志不渝，团结带领人民历经千难万险，付出巨大牺牲，敢于面对曲折，勇于修正错误，攻克了一个又一个看似不可攻克的难关，创造了一个又一个彪炳史册的人间奇迹。

The Original Aspiration and the Mission of the CPC

The original aspiration and the mission of Chinese Communists is to seek happiness for the Chinese people and rejuvenation for the Chinese nation. This original aspiration, this mission, is what inspires Chinese Communists to advance.

Only by bearing in mind why we started, can we move toward our goal. Over the past 90-plus years, to accomplish the historic mission of national rejuvenation, whether in times of weakness or strength, whether in times of adversity or smooth sailing, the CPC has never forgotten its founding mission, nor wavered in its pursuit. It has united the people and led them in conquering countless challenges, making enormous sacrifices, meeting setbacks squarely, and courageously righting wrongs. Thus we have, time and again, overcome the seemingly insurmountable and created miracle upon miracle.

新的历史特点的伟大斗争

中共十九大报告指出，实现伟大梦想，必须进行伟大斗争。中国共产党要团结带领人民有效应对重大挑战、抵御重大风险、克服重大阻力、解决重大矛盾，必须进行具有许多新的历史特点的伟大斗争。有矛盾就有斗争，有斗争才有发展。中国共产党的历史就是一部斗争史。伟大斗争是实现伟大梦想的行动措施、方式手段、精神状态，更是一种勇气、一种品质、一种价值观、一种责任担当，在“四个伟大”（伟大斗争、伟大工程、伟大事业、伟大梦想）中起变革性、创新性作用。具有许多新的历史特点的伟大斗争，不同于革命战争年代那种疾风骤雨式的阶级斗争，也不是社会主义建设初期那种大规模的群众运动，而是为发展中国特色社会主义进行的一系列伟大创新创造，是为了实现中华民族伟大复兴的中国梦而实施的战略举措、突破遏制、回应挑战、补齐短板的斗争。

A Great Struggle That Responds to Contemporary Realities

As the report to the 19th CPC National Congress puts it, it takes a great struggle to make our great dream come true. To be able to lead the people in a joint effort to overcome formidable challenges, risks and barriers, the CPC must undertake a great struggle that responds to contemporary realities.

It takes uphill struggles to surmount daunting obstacles and lead to progress. The history of the CPC is a history of struggle. A great struggle is inevitable if we intend to make our great dream a reality. It is the only means to achieve our goal. It reflects our mental preparedness, our courage, our determination, our values, and our sense of responsibility. It is transformative and innovative in nature, and unfolds in lockstep with what we call a great struggle, a great project, a great cause, and a great dream.

Unlike a class struggle in the turbulent era of the revolutionary war or a mass movement in the early days of socialism, today's great struggle represents a series of innovative moves aimed at developing socialism with Chinese characteristics, and embodies our strategy to bring about the great rejuvenation of the Chinese nation. It is a struggle to thwart containment, to confront challenges, and to address weaknesses.

党的建设新的伟大工程

实现伟大梦想，必须建设伟大工程。这个伟大工程就是我们党正在深入推进的党的建设新的伟大工程。历史已经并将继续证明，没有中国共产党的领导，民族复兴必然是空想。中国共产党领导，是中国特色社会主义最本质的特征，是中国特色社会主义制度的最大优势，也是实现中华民族伟大复兴这一历史使命的最大政治保障。伟大斗争、伟大工程、伟大事业、伟大梦想，紧密联系、相互贯通、相互作用，其中起决定性作用的是党的建设新的伟大工程。

当前，中国共产党面临的执政环境是复杂的，影响党的先进性、弱化党的纯洁性的因素也是复杂的，党内存在的思想不纯、组织不纯、作风不纯等突出问题尚未得到根本解决。统筹推进“四个伟大”，必须强化伟大工程这个根本性政治保证，毫不动摇坚持和完善党的领导，毫不动摇把党建设得更加坚强有力，确保党永葆旺盛生命力和强大战斗力，把党建设成为始终走在时代前列、人民衷心拥护、勇于自我

A New Great Project of Party Building

Realizing our great dream demands a great project. This project is the great new project of Party building that is just getting into full swing. As history has shown and will continue to bear witness to, without the leadership of the Communist Party of China, national rejuvenation would be just wishful thinking.

Leadership by the CPC is the defining feature of socialism with Chinese characteristics, the greatest strength of our distinctly Chinese socialist system, and the strongest guarantee of a successful historic mission of bringing about national rejuvenation. This great project and what we call a great struggle, a great cause and a great dream are interrelated and mutually supportive, with the great project playing a decisive role.

As a ruling party, the CPC is now facing complex challenges, which may erode its advanced nature and purity. Many ideological and organizational flaws and unwholesome tendencies are still plaguing our Party.

Greater efforts are called for to implement our great project as a fundamental pillar of political support for our great struggle, great cause and great dream. We must unwaveringly reaffirm the Party's leadership role and make the Party still stronger through

革命、经得起各种风浪考验、朝气蓬勃的马克思主义执政党；必须推动全面从严治党向纵深发展，围绕加强党的长期执政能力建设、先进性和纯洁性建设为主线，以党的政治建设为统领，以坚定理想信念宗旨为根基，全面推进党的政治建设、思想建设、组织建设、作风建设、纪律建设，把制度建设贯穿其中，深入推进反腐败斗争，不断提高党的建设质量；必须结合伟大斗争、伟大事业、伟大梦想的实践来推进党的建设新的伟大工程，确保党始终走在时代前列，始终成为全国人民的主心骨，始终成为坚强领导核心，始终总揽全局、协调各方。

Party development measures, so as to build a Marxist governing party with a vibrant organizational culture, a party that is always ready to answer the call of the times, enjoys the support of the people, has the courage to reform itself, and is able to withstand all tests. The campaign to enforce strict Party discipline must proceed at a deeper level. The Party's long-term governance capacity must be strengthened, and its advanced nature and purity protected, through political awareness initiatives based on the Party's ideals, convictions, and fundamental goals. An all-round push for Party development incorporates political awareness, organizational improvement, ethical issues, discipline enforcement, and institution building. Anti-corruption measures must be strengthened to improve the efficacy of Party development. The great project must be implemented in tandem with our great struggle, great cause and great dream to ensure the Party's ability to always stay ahead of time, to provide cohesion and overall guidance, and to lead and coordinate.

中国特色社会主义伟大事业

实现伟大梦想，必须推进伟大事业。伟大的梦想指引伟大的事业，伟大的事业成就伟大的梦想。中国特色社会主义是改革开放以来党的全部理论和实践的主题，是党和人民历尽千辛万苦、付出巨大代价取得的根本成就。中国特色社会主义道路是实现社会主义现代化、创造人民美好生活的必由之路，中国特色社会主义理论体系是指导党和人民实现中华民族伟大复兴的正确理论，中国特色社会主义制度是当代中国发展进步的根本制度保障，中国特色社会主义文化是激励全党全国各族人民奋勇前进的强大精神力量。全党要更加自觉地增强道路自信、理论自信、制度自信、文化自信，既不走封闭僵化的老路，也不走改旗易帜的邪路，保持政治定力，坚持实干兴邦，始终坚持和发展中国特色社会主义。在“四个伟大”中，伟大事业

A Great Cause of Socialism with Chinese Characteristics

To make our great dream come true, we must pursue our great cause of socialism with Chinese characteristics. Our great dream guides our great cause, which aims to realize our dream.

Socialism with Chinese characteristics has been the central theme of all of the Party's theories and programs since reform and opening up began. It is what defines the fundamental achievement that our Party and our people have made by overcoming countless hardships at an enormous cost.

The path of socialism with Chinese characteristics is the only path to socialist modernization and a better life for the people.

The theory of socialism with Chinese characteristics is what guides the Party and people in a joint effort to achieve national rejuvenation.

The socialist system with Chinese characteristics provides an institutional fulcrum for China's march toward a better future.

The culture of socialism with Chinese characteristics is a powerful source of strength that inspires all members of the Party and the people of all ethnic groups to move forward.

It is essential to strengthen our confidence

是旗帜方向和道路途径，起全局性、引领性作用。进入新时代，只有不断推进中国特色社会主义伟大事业，才能逐步实现中华民族复兴的伟大梦想。

in the path we take, the theory that guides us forward, the political system we choose, and the culture we nurture. We cannot afford to go back to the old days of self-imposed isolation when ideological rigidity reigned, nor can we change our course and abandon our founding mission. We must remain steadfast in upholding and developing socialism with Chinese characteristics, and focusing on results-oriented initiatives to create greater prosperity.

“四个自信”

2016年7月1日，习近平在庆祝中国共产党成立95周年大会上的讲话中，在“三个自信”（道路自信、理论自信、制度自信）基础上，增加了“文化自信”，从而形成了“四个自信”的表述。“四个自信”的概括是对中国特色社会主义理论体系的丰富和创新。其中，道路自信是对中国特色社会主义道路发展方向和未来命运的自信；理论自信是对中国特色社会主义理论体系的科学性、真理性、正确性的自信；制度自信是对中国特色社会主义制度先进性和优越性的自信；文化自信是对中国自身文化价值的充分肯定，是对自身文化生命力的坚定信念。“四个自信”是一个有机统一体，是中国特色社会主义的完整信念体系，相辅相成、彼此互动。其中，文化自信是更基础、更广泛、更深厚的自信，是更基本、更深沉、更持久的力量。在5000多年文明发展中孕育的中华优秀传统文化，在党和人民伟大斗争中孕育的革命文化和社会主义先进文化，积淀着中华民族最深层的精神追求，代表着中华民族

"Four Matters of Confidence"

In his speech of July 1, 2016, at the celebration of the 95th anniversary of the founding of the Chinese Communist Party, Xi Jinping added "confidence in its culture" to the existing "three matters of confidence" (the socialist path, theory and system), thus coining the term "four matters of confidence." The scope of this term is an augmentation of and innovation in the theoretical system of socialism with Chinese characteristics.

"Confidence in its path" is confidence in the direction of development of socialism with Chinese characteristics and confidence in its future; "confidence in its theory" is confidence in the scientific, true and authentic nature of the theory of socialism with Chinese characteristics; "confidence in its system" is confidence in the advanced and superior nature of the system of Chinese socialism; "confidence in its culture" is a full affirmation of the value of China's own culture and a faith in its vitality.

These four form an organic whole; they provide a complete conceptual system of socialism with Chinese characteristics; they are mutually complementary and interactive. Of the four, "confidence in its culture" is the most fundamental, profound, broad, basic, deep-rooted, and longest-lasting. China's outstanding traditional culture took shape

独特的精神标识。坚定中国特色社会主义道路自信、理论自信、制度自信、文化自信，不断夺取中国特色社会主义新胜利，是当代中国共产党人最核心的使命。

over the course of 5,000 years of development of its civilization. Its revolutionary culture and advanced socialist culture were formed through great struggles of the Party and the people. The Chinese culture, crystallizing the deepest aspirations, embodies the distinctive traits of the Chinese spirit.

The most important core mission of today's Communist Party members is to remain firmly confident in the path, theory, system and culture of socialism with Chinese characteristics, and to continually raise it to new heights.

决胜全面建成小康社会，开启全面建设社会主义现代化国家新征程

Completing the Building of a Moderately Prosperous Society in All Respects

“两个一百年”奋斗目标

中共十八大描绘了全面建成小康社会、加快推进社会主义现代化的宏伟蓝图，发出了向“两个一百年”奋斗目标前进的时代号召。该奋斗目标是，到 2021 年中国共产党成立一百年时全面建成小康社会，国内生产总值和城乡居民人均收入比 2010 年翻一番；到2049年中华人民共和国成立一百年时建成富强民主文明和谐美丽的社会主义现代化强国。这一目标，既是中华民族的宏伟目标，也把每个人、每个家庭、各方面群众的愿望和利益结合起来。这一奋斗目标将中国梦的蓝图和光明前景具体化，成为实现中国梦的基础。实现这一目标，对中国这样一个拥有13亿多人口、发展还不平衡的国家来说并非易事，必须坚持以经济建设为中心，需要继续长期艰苦奋斗。从十九大到二十大，是“两个一百年”奋斗目标的历史交汇期。我

The Two Centennial Goals

The Two Centennial Goals were portrayed at the 18th National Congress of the CPC, which unveiled a roadmap for completing the building of a moderately prosperous society and accelerating socialist modernization.

Specifically, the first goal calls for completing the building of a moderately prosperous society, and doubling China's 2010 GDP and per capita income, by the time the CPC celebrates its centenary in 2021, and the second goal calls for building China into a modern socialist country that is prosperous, strong, democratic, culturally advanced, harmonious and beautiful, by the time the People's Republic celebrates its centenary in 2049.

Ambitious on a national level, these goals also reflect the wishes and expectations of individuals, families and communities. They embody the grand vision and ideals the Chinese Dream represents, and their realization paves the way for making the Chinese Dream a reality. It is however a tall order to achieve these goals for a country like China with a population of more than 1.3 billion and uneven levels of development across regions. Sustained long-term efforts are needed, with an unswerving focus on economic

们既要全面建成小康社会、实现第一个百年奋斗目标，又要乘势而上开启全面建设社会主义现代化国家新征程，向第二个百年奋斗目标进军。

development.

The period between the 19th and the 20th national congresses of the CPC is the period in which the timeframes of the Two Centennial Goals converge. In this period, not only must China complete the building of a moderately prosperous society in all respects and achieve the first centennial goal; it must also build on this achievement to embark on a new journey toward the second centennial goal of building a modern socialist country in every dimension.

科教兴国战略

1995年5月，中共中央、国务院召开全国科学技术大会，决定在全国实施科教兴国战略。20多年以来，“九五”计划、2010年远景目标等一系列重大决策部署不断赋予其新内涵。党的十九大报告更是将科教兴国战略确定为决胜全面建成小康社会需要坚定实施的七大战略之一，“科教兴国”被赋予新的时代内涵。科教兴国战略就是在“科学技术是第一生产力”思想的指导下，坚持教育为本，把科技和教育摆在经济、社会发展的重要位置，增强国家的科技实力和科学技术向现实生产力转化的能力，提高科技对经济的贡献率，提高全民族的科技文化素质，把经济建设转移到依靠科技进步和提高劳动者素质的轨道上来，加速实现国家的繁荣昌盛。

科教兴国战略，基础在教育，关键在科技。实施科教兴国战略，既要充分发挥科技和教育在兴国中的作用，又要努力培植科技和教育这个兴国的基础。实施科教兴国战略，必须深化科技和教育体制改革，促进科技、教育同经济的结合。

Strategy for Invigorating China Through Science and Education

The strategy for invigorating China through science and education was unveiled by the Party Central Committee and the State Council at the National Conference on Science and Technology in May 1995. It has been enriched with the infusion of new insights contained in a series of policies rolled out in the past 20 years, including the Ninth Five-year Plan and Vision 2010. It is highlighted in the report to the 19th CPC National Congress as one of the seven strategies for completing the building of a moderately prosperous society, and incorporates new directives that respond to today's new challenges.

The strategy for invigorating China through science and education is guided by the thinking that science and technology is a primary source of productivity growth. It emphasizes the importance of education and science and technology in promoting economic and social development, and the need for strengthened capacity building in science and technology and for expanded application of science and technology to productivity growth, so as to increase the contribution of science and technology to the economy. The strategy also aims to raise public awareness and understanding

科技工作必须自觉面向经济建设主战场，将攻克国民经济发展中迫切需要解决的关键问题作为主要任务；教育工作要面向现代化、面向世界、面向未来，优化教育结构，改革教育体制，合理配置资源，提高教育质量和办学效益，使教育与经济紧密结合起来。

of science and technology, as part of the effort to increase the reliance of economic development on science and technology and to promote human development, a move that helps accelerate China's march toward greater prosperity.

This strategy relies on education. The key to its successful implementation is the development of science and technology. To ensure that science and technology plays its due role in economic development, it is essential to promote the development of education and science and technology.

To this end, further institutional reform is necessary in education and in the field of science and technology, and better alignment is called for between education and science and technology on the one hand and the economy in general on the other. Science and technology initiatives should be better geared toward economic development, and focus more on tackling urgent issues that bear on economic development. Education should be oriented toward our modernization drive and toward the future, with greater openness to the outside world. Structural reform in education should proceed in tandem with measures to rationalize resource allocation, so as to improve education quality and efficiency and to ensure that education better serves the economy.

人才强国战略

2002年5月，中共中央下发《2002-2005年全国人才队伍建设规划纲要》，提出实施人才强国战略。2007年，人才强国战略作为发展中国特色社会主义的三大基本战略之一写入《中国共产党党章》和党的十七大报告；2017年，党的十九大报告将人才强国战略确定为决胜全面建成小康社会需要坚定实施的七大战略之一。

人才强国与科教兴国并列存在，两者相辅相成，不可分割。人才强国战略的核心是人才兴国，工作重心是建设人才资源强国，充分发挥人才的作用。党的十九大报告提出，坚持党管人才原则，聚天下英才而用之，加快建设人才强国；实行更加积极、更加开放、更加有效的人才政策，以识才的慧眼、爱才的诚意、用才的胆识、容才的雅量、聚才的良方，把党内和党外、国内和国外各方面优秀人才聚集到党和人民的伟大奋斗中来，鼓励引导人才向边远地区、边疆民族地区、革命老区和基层一线流动，努力形成人人渴望成才、人人努力成才、人人皆可成才、人人尽展其才的良好局面，让各类人才的创造活力

Strategy to Make China a Talent-Strong Country

A national plan of action to develop a quality workforce (2002-2005) was launched by the Party Central Committee in May 2002. Talent development was included in the Party Constitution and the report to the 17th National Congress in 2007 as one of the three basic strategies. It was also incorporated in the report to the 19th National Congress in 2017 as one of the seven strategies for completing the process of building a moderately prosperous society.

Talent development and the development of education and science and technology are inseparable and mutually reinforcing. Our talent strategy focuses on the need to expand our talent pool and better use talent to advance toward our goal of building a prosperous country.

In his report to the 19th CPC National Congress, Xi Jinping emphasized the Party's leadership role in talent development, and the need to attract talent from far and near and to make China a talent-strong country. It is important to have in place a more proactive, open, and effective talent policy that guides talent identification, recruitment and retention, and encourages bold moves and competitive measures to welcome much needed experts in various fields into our team from inside and

竞相迸发、聪明才智充分涌流。作为国家发展战略，人才强国战略与国家发展的战略目标高度协调一致，将为实现全面建成小康社会和实现中华民族伟大复兴的“中国梦”提供人才保证和智力支持。

outside the Party and from China and other countries. It is also important to encourage skilled personnel to work in small communities, remote areas, border regions with mainly ethnic minority populations, and old revolutionary base areas. A favorable talent development culture is needed to inspire everyone to discover and develop his or her own talent and to realize his or her full potential, so that together we will unleash our collective creativity.

As part of our national development strategy, our talent development strategy is fully in line with national strategic development goals and by ensuring talent supply, supports efforts to complete the building of a moderately prosperous society and realize our dream of national rejuvenation.

创新驱动发展战略

2012年11月召开的中共十八大作出了实施创新驱动发展战略的重大部署。创新始终是推动一个国家、一个民族向前发展的重要力量。实施创新驱动发展战略决定着中华民族前途命运。中国是一个发展中大国，正在大力推进经济发展方式转变和经济结构调整，必须把创新驱动发展战略实施好。“十三五”规划明确提出了“深入实施创新驱动发展战略”。2016年5月，中共中央、国务院印发了《国家创新驱动发展战略纲要》。中国实施创新驱动发展战略，就是要推动以科技创新为核心的全面创新，坚持需求导向和产业化方向，坚持企业在创新中的主体地位，发挥市场在资源配置中的决定性作用和社会主义制度优势，增强科技进步对经济增长的贡献度，形成新的增长动力源泉，推动经济持续健康发展。实施创新驱动发展战略最为紧迫的是要进一步解放思想，加快科技体制改革步伐，破除一切束缚创新驱动发展的观念和体制机制障碍。实施创新驱动发展战略是一项系统工程，涉及方方面面的工作。实施创新驱动发展战略的主要措施包

The Innovation-Driven Development Strategy

In November 2012, at its 18th National Congress, the CPC made a series of important decisions on the implementation of the innovation-driven development strategy. As innovation has always offered important impetus to the progress of a country and a nation, an innovation-driven development strategy has a significant bearing on the future of the Chinese nation.

China is a large developing country which is pushing to transform its development model and economic structure, therefore it must make sure that the innovation-driven development strategy is implemented properly and successfully. For this purpose, the 13th Five-year Plan contains extensive measures for its implementation, and the CPC Central Committee and the State Council issued in May 2016 Outlines on National Strategy for Innovation Driven Development. China's innovation-driven development strategy aims at encouraging innovation in all areas, led by scientific and technological innovation.

Innovation should be demand-driven in response to the needs of industrialization, and businesses are major players in delivering innovation. The market should play the decisive role in allocating resources, and the full potential of our socialist system should be

括：营造激励创新的公平竞争环境，建立技术创新市场导向机制，强化金融创新的功能，完善成果转化激励政策，构建更加高效的科研体系，创新培养、用好和吸引人才机制，推动形成深度融合的开放创新局面等等。中国将力争到2020年，基本形成适应创新驱动发展要求的制度环境和政策法律体系，为进入创新型国家行列提供有力保障。

tapped. The strategy also seeks to enhance the contribution of scientific and technological advances to economic growth, which will serve as a new growth driver and help sustain sound economic development. As we implement the innovation-driven development strategy, we must open our minds and accelerate the reform of the science and technology system so that we can free ourselves from the stereotyped thinking and institutional barriers that hinder innovation-driven development.

The strategy must be implemented in a systematic manner involving efforts in different areas. The main measures to be taken to this end include creating a favorable environment for fair competition with a market-based mechanism that encourages technological innovation. It is also essential to promote financial innovation to provide more incentives for innovative uses of technology.

Another area of focus is building a more efficient scientific research system, and implementing an effective talent management mechanism for training and attracting competent personnel. A highly-integrated approach is necessary to ensure an open and innovation-friendly climate.

China seeks to have in place by 2020 an institutional, legal and policy framework for innovation-driven development so as to provide a solid basis to put China on track to become one of the world's most innovative countries.

乡村振兴战略

21世纪以来，中共中央持续加大对农村的扶持力度，坚持把农业、农村、农民问题作为党工作的重中之重。从2003年起，连续15年中央一号文件均聚焦于农业、农村、农民（即“三农”）问题。中共十七大和十八大也分别提出城乡统筹和城乡一体化的发展思路，对于推动农村发展、增加农民收入起到重要作用。同时，我国最大的发展不平衡，仍然是城乡发展不平衡；最大的发展不充分，仍然是农村发展的不充分。党的十九大报告首次提出实施乡村振兴战略的新发展理念，并将其确定为决胜全面建成小康社会需要坚定实施的七大战略之一。

乡村振兴战略强调，要坚持农业农村

Strategy for Rural Revitalization

Since the beginning of the 21st century, the Party Central Committee has continued to step up its support for rural communities. Issues concerning agriculture, rural development and the wellbeing of farmers now top the agenda of the Party. In the past 15 years, the first document issued by the central authority during each calendar year since 2003 had a rural focus. Plans for integrated urban-rural development were proposed in the reports to the 17th and 18th CPC national congresses, providing an important boost to agricultural development and farmers' income.

Meanwhile, the urban-rural imbalance remains the most serious imbalance, and rural development remains the most serious development challenge. A rural revitalization strategy was thus unveiled for the first time in the report to the 19th CPC National Congress as one of the seven strategies for reaching the goal of building a moderately prosperous society.

The strategy emphasizes the importance of rural development, including the need to develop rural businesses, create a pleasant living environment, promote civility and effective governance, and improve the living standards of rural residents. To this end, enabling mechanisms and policies are needed to

优先发展，按照产业兴旺、生态宜居、乡风文明、治理有效、生活富裕的总要求，建立健全城乡融合发展体制机制和政策体系，加快推进农业农村现代化。乡村振兴的关键和重点是产业振兴。实施乡村振兴战略需要全面深化农村改革，巩固和完善农村基本经营制度，深化农村土地制度改革，完善承包地“三权”分置制度；保持土地承包关系稳定并长久不变，第二轮土地承包到期后再延长三十年；深化农村集体产权制度改革，保障农民财产权益，壮大集体经济；确保国家粮食安全，把中国人的饭碗牢牢端在自己手中；构建现代农业产业体系、生产体系、经营体系，完善农业支持保护制度，发展多种形式适度规模经营，培育新型农业经营主体，健全农业社会化服务体系，实现小农户和现代农业发展有机衔接。实施乡村振兴战略的同时也需要有强大的科技和人才支撑，为此

promote integrated urban-rural development, and speed up agricultural and rural modernization. The key to rural revitalization is developing rural businesses.

The strategy calls for in-depth rural reform to improve the basic rural economic structure. Especially important is rural land tenure reform aimed at separating ownership rights, contract rights, and management rights. Rural land contracting practices will remain unchanged; and existing contracts will be extended for another 30 years upon expiration. Reform of the rural collective ownership system will proceed to safeguard property rights of rural residents, and strengthen the collective economy.

It is crucial to always have control over our own food supply so as to ensure China's food security. We will establish or improve mechanisms that encourage the development of modern rural businesses, promote agricultural production and best management practices, and provide support and protection for agriculture. It is also important to encourage the development of various types of economies of scale, modernize the rural structure, improve specialized agricultural services, and better align smallholder farming and the development of modern agriculture.

Rural revitalization would not materialize without the support of science and technology or without effective talent management. Integrated development of industry, agriculture and the service sector is essential in rural areas. We will support and encourage

要促进农村一二三产业融合发展，支持和鼓励农民就业创业，拓宽增收渠道；加强农村基层基础工作，健全自治、法治、德治相结合的乡村治理体系；培养造就一支懂农业、爱农村、爱农民的“三农”工作队伍。

employment creation and entrepreneurship, and promote and encourage more income generating activities. It is important to strengthen basic services in rural communities, and improve rural governance by improving self-governance mechanisms and promoting the rule of law and ethical standards. It is also important to build a team of rural development professionals well versed in agricultural science and having an affinity with rural areas and the people there.

区域协调发展战略

区域协调发展战略是我国经济社会发展战略的重要组成部分。新世纪以来，我国逐步形成西部开发、东北振兴、中部崛起、东部率先发展的区域发展总体战略。中共十九大报告明确提出区域协调发展战略，并将区域协调发展战略确定为决胜全面建成小康社会需要坚定实施的七大战略之一。

今后一个时期实施区域协调发展战略的任务主要包括：加大力度支持革命老区、民族地区、边疆地区、贫困地区加快发展，强化举措推进西部大开发形成新格局，深化改革加快东北等老工业基地振兴，发挥优势推动中部地区崛起，创新引领率先实现东部地区优化发展，建立更加有效的区域协调发展新机制。以城市群为主体构建大中小城市和小城镇协调发展的城镇格局，加快农业转移人口市民化；以疏解北京非首都功能为“牛鼻子”推动京津冀协同发展，高起点规划、高标准建设雄安新区；以共抓大保护、不搞大开发为导向推动长江经济带发展，支持资源型地

Strategy for Coordinated Regional Development

A coordinated subnational regional development strategy is an important component of our economic and social development strategy. Since the beginning of the 21st century, an overall strategy has gradually taken shape, focusing on the development of the western region, the revitalization of the northeast, the takeoff of the central region, and the leading role of the eastern region. Such a strategy was highlighted in the report to the 19th CPC National Congress as one of the seven strategies for realizing the goal of building a moderately prosperous society.

The tasks to implement the strategy for coordinated regional development in the coming years include:

• expanding support for old revolutionary base areas, areas with large ethnic minority populations, border regions, and economically disadvantaged areas;

• stepping up large-scale development efforts in the western region;

• pursuing reform at a deeper level to accelerate the revitalization of old industrial bases in the northeast and other parts of the country;

• boosting the rise of the central region by tapping into local strengths;

• supporting the pioneering role of the eastern region in innovation-driven

区经济转型发展；加快边疆发展，确保边疆巩固、边境安全；坚持陆海统筹，加快建设海洋强国。

区域协调发展战略是对“两个一百年”奋斗目标历史交汇期中国区域发展的新部署，对中国增强区域发展协同性、拓展区域发展新空间、推动建设现代化经济体系、实现“两个一百年”奋斗目标均具有重大战略意义。

development; and creating new, effective mechanisms to facilitate inter-regional coordination.

A network of city clusters has been envisaged, in order to enable better coordination among cities of different sizes and small towns in responding to their development needs. Plans are being implemented to speed up the process of granting permanent urban residency to rural migrant workers. All functions nonessential to its role as the nation's capital will be relocated from Beijing to neighboring locations as part of the effort to drive coordinated development of the Beijing-Tianjin-Hebei region. The Xiong'an New Area in the vicinity of Beijing is being developed to high standards laid out in forward-looking plans. Also underway are eco-friendly initiatives for the Yangtze Economic Belt, which promote coordination in environmental conservation and are against excessive development. Support will be given to resource-dependent areas to help transform their local economies. Development in border regions will be accelerated, and stability and security there must be protected. An integrated approach to land and marine management is vital to the efforts to build China into a strong maritime country.

The strategy for coordinated regional development was launched at a critical juncture for the realization of the Two Centennial Goals. It is of strategic importance to strengthening China's subnational development coordination, expanding regional development opportunities, building a modern economic system, and realizing the Two Centennial Goals.

可持续发展战略

我国是人口众多、资源相对不足的国家。改革开放以来，党中央、国务院高度重视中国的可持续发展。1994年3月，国务院通过《中国21世纪议程》，确定实施可持续发展战略。2003年初，国务院颁布《中国21世纪初可持续发展行动纲要》，明确未来10到20年的可持续发展目标、重点和保障措施。中共十五大、十六大、十七大、十八大，都对可持续发展战略提出新要求。可持续发展战略事关中华民族的长远发展，事关子孙后代福祉，具有全局性、根本性、长期性。党的十九大报告将可持续发展战略确定为决胜全面建成小康社会需要坚定实施的七大战略之一。可持续发展是基于社会、经济、人口、资源、环境相互协调和共同发展的理论和战略，主要包括生态可持续发展、经济可持续发展和社会可持续发展，以保护自然资源环境为基础，以激励经济发展为条件，以改善和提高人类生活质量为目标，宗旨是既能相对满足当代人的需求，又不能对后代的发展构成危害。中国实施可持续发展战略的指导思想是坚持以人为本，以人与自

Strategy for Sustainable Development

China has a large population and limited resources. Ever since the policy of reform and opening up was initiated, the Party Central Committee and the State Council have been attaching great importance to the issue of sustainable development. *China's Agenda 21* adopted by the State Council in March 1994 reconfirmed the imperative to promote sustainable development. A program of action on sustainable development in the early 21st century unveiled by the State Council in early 2003 outlined sustainable development goals, areas of focus and measures to achieve these goals in the following 10 to 20 years. New sustainable development measures were also proposed at the 15th, 16th, 17th and 18th CPC national congresses. Sustainable development is key to the survival of our nation and to the wellbeing of generations to come. It is a cross-cutting, long-term issue of fundamental importance. A sustainable development strategy was identified in the report to the 19th CPC National Congress as one of the seven strategies for realizing the goal of building a moderately prosperous society.

Underpinning this strategy is the concept of coordination and interaction between social, economic, demographic and environmental forces. The strategy covers ecological,

然的和谐为主线，以经济发展为核心，以提高人民群众生活质量为根本出发点，以科技和体制创新为突破口，坚持不懈地全面推进经济社会与人口、资源和生态环境的协调，不断提高中国的综合国力和竞争力。十九大报告赋予可持续发展战略新的时代内涵，首次提出建设“富强民主文明和谐美丽”的社会主义现代化强国目标，生态文明建设上升为新时代中国特色社会主义的重要组成部分。

economic and social sustainability. It promotes economic development while protecting natural resources and the environment. It aims to improve the wellbeing of the people, and to ensure that the needs of the present generation are met without compromising the chance and potential of future generations.

The strategy is informed by a people-centered approach, a vision for harmony between man and nature, and the need for eco-friendly economic development. Science and technology and institutional reform will play a critical role in improving the wellbeing of the people. We must never falter in our efforts to strike a balance between economic, social, demographic, resource and environmental considerations, while strengthening China's composite national strength and competitiveness.

By placing the sustainable development strategy in a new context, the report to the 19th CPC National Congress outlined for the first time the goal of building a great modern socialist country that is prosperous, strong, democratic, culturally advanced, harmonious, and beautiful. Environmental protection has thus become an important element of socialism with Chinese characteristics for a new era.

军民融合发展战略

2015年3月，习近平出席十二届全国人大三次会议解放军代表团全体会议时提出，“把军民融合发展上升为国家战略”；同年10月的中共十八届五中全会上明确提出，“实施军民融合发展战略，形成全要素、多领域、高效益的军民深度融合发展格局”，这被认为是中国长期探索经济建设和国防建设协调发展规律的重大成果。实施军民融合发展战略，关键在于统筹经济建设和国防建设，使经济建设与国防建设相互促进、相互支撑，实现富国和强军的统一。为了实施好该战略，“十三五”期间，中国一方面将在国家层面加强顶层设计，把国防和军队建设规划的宏观需求纳入经济社会发展规划，并完善配套政策法规制度，加大法规建设力度。另一方面

Strategy for National Military-Civilian Integration

Addressing the plenary meeting of the military delegates to the Third Session of the 12th National People's Congress in March 2015, Xi Jinping announced a plan to step up military-civilian integration as part of a national strategy. At its fifth plenary session in October 2015, the 18th CPC Central Committee decided to implement a strategy of building an extensive and efficient multi-sector structure for integrating military and civilian resources. This was seen as a major step toward strengthened coordination between economic development and the efforts to build a strong military.

The key to effectively implementing the strategy is an integration of economic and national defense priorities, to create synergy so that efforts on both fronts become complementary to each other and mutually reinforcing. During the period covered by the 13th Five-year Plan (2016-2020), planning at the top level will be intensified to incorporate national defense and military needs into an overall economic and social development framework. At the same time, related regulatory policies and legal mechanisms will be fine-tuned. It is also necessary to introduce competition into the defense industry by

也将引入竞争激发活力，打破军工垄断体制、降低民企准入门槛、强化安全保密监管，确保资源投入有质量有效益。

breaking the monopoly of defense enterprises and improving market access for civilian businesses, while guaranteeing security, confidentiality, quality and cost-effectiveness.

国家治理体系和治理能力现代化

2013年11月召开的中共十八届三中全会提出，全面深化改革的总目标是完善和发展中国特色社会主义制度，推进国家治理体系和治理能力现代化。国家治理体系和治理能力是一个国家制度和制度执行能力的集中体现。国家治理体系是在党领导下管理国家的制度体系，包括经济、政治、文化、社会、生态文明和党的建设等各领域体制机制、法律法规安排，也就是一整套紧密相连、相互协调的国家制度；国家治理能力则是运用国家制度管理社会各方面事务的能力，包括改革发展稳定、内政外交国防、治党治国治军等各个方面。国家治理体系和治理能力是一个有机整体，相辅相成，有了好的国家治理体系才能提高治理能力，提高国家治理能力才能充分发挥国家治理体系的效能。推进国家治理体系和治理能力现代化，就是要适应时代变化，既改革不适应实践发展要求的体制机制、法律法规，又不断构建新的体制机制、法律法规，使各方面制度更

Modernizing the National Governance System and Capacity

At its third plenary session, which was held on November 9-12, 2013, the 18th CPC Central Committee stated that the overarching goal of comprehensively expanding in-depth reform is to refine and develop socialism with Chinese characteristics, and to modernize the national governance system and capacity. The governance system and capacity of a country are embodied in its institutions and its ability to execute the institutions.

China's national governance system, led by the Party, is a system of institutions for managing the country. These include economic, political, cultural, social, ecological and Party development mechanisms and institutions, as well as laws, regulations and plans. These are a complete set of tightly linked and coordinated national institutions.

China's national governance capacity are defined by its ability to use these institutions to manage various aspects of society, including reform, development and stability; internal affairs, foreign relations and national defense; and governance of the Party, the nation and the armed forces.

The governance system and capacity are mutually complementary and holistically integrated; there must be a good governance

加科学、更加完善，实现党、国家、社会各项事务治理制度化、规范化、程序化。要更加注重治理能力建设，增强按制度办事、依法办事意识，善于运用制度和法律治理国家，把各方面制度优势转化为管理国家的效能，提高党科学执政、民主执政、依法执政水平。推进国家治理体系和治理能力现代化，是完善和发展中国特色社会主义制度的必然要求，是实现社会主义现代化的应有之义。

system in order to improve governance capacity, and capacity must be improved if the system is to be fully effective. Promoting their modernization means adapting to changing times and reforming institutions, laws and regulations which are unsuited to the needs of development, while at the same time constantly establishing new institutions, laws and regulations, so that all institutions become efficient and complete, thereby making the governance of the Party, of the nation and of the society more institutionalized, more standardized and more procedure-oriented.

More emphasis must be given to strengthening governance capacity:

• Work must be done according to more clearly-defined institutional guidelines;

• There must be a stronger awareness of acting in accordance with the law;

• We must be adept at using institutions and laws to manage the country;

• All institutional strengths should become national governance capacities; and

• The Party's ability to govern systematically, democratically and in accordance with the law must be improved.

Modernizing the national governance system and capacity is a requirement for refining and developing Chinese socialism, and it is necessary for achieving socialist modernization.

贯彻新发展理念，建设现代化经济体系

Applying a New Vision of Development and Developing a Modernized Economy

建设现代化经济体系

中共十九大报告首次明确提出建设现代化经济体系。新中国成立后，我国逐步建立了独立的比较完整的国民经济体系。当前，中国经济已由高速增长阶段转向高质量发展阶段，正处在转变发展方式、优化经济结构、转换增长动力的攻关期，建设现代化经济体系，是开启全面建设社会主义现代化国家新征程的重大任务；是解决我国社会主要矛盾客观要求；是跨越关口的迫切要求和我国发展的战略目标。

必须坚持质量第一、效益优先，以供给侧结构性改革为主线，推动经济发展质量变革、效率变革、动力变革，提高全要素生产率，着力加快建设实体经济、科技创新、现代金融、人力资源协同发展的产业体系，着力构建市场机制有效、微观主体有活力、宏观调控有度的经济体制，不断增强我国经济创新力和竞争力。建设现代化经济体系，需要落实六大战略举措：一是深化供给侧结构性改革，二是加快建设创新型国家，三是实施乡村振兴战略，四是实施区域协调发展战略，五是加快完

Developing a Modernized Economy

A plan for developing a modernized economy was first unveiled in the report to the 19th CPC National Congress. Since the founding of the People's Republic of China, an independent and diversified economy has gradually taken shape. China's economy has currently been transitioning from rapid growth to quality-oriented development. This is a pivotal stage for transforming our growth model, improving our economic structure, and fostering new drivers of growth. It is imperative to develop a modernized economy as part of the effort to build a modern socialist country and to overcome major challenges we now face. This is what has to be urgently accomplished in order to get us through this critical transition, and is of strategic importance to China's future development.

We must put quality first and give priority to performance. We should pursue supply-side structural reform as our main task, and work hard for better quality, higher efficiency, and more robust drivers of economic growth through reform. We need to raise total factor productivity and accelerate the building of an industrial system that promotes coordinated development of the real economy with technological innovation, modern finance, and human resources. We should endeavor

善社会主义市场经济体制，六是推动形成全面开放新格局。总之，建设现代化经济体系就是要贯彻新发展理念，努力实现更高质量、更有效率、更加公平、更可持续的发展。

to develop an economy with more effective market mechanisms, dynamic micro-entities, and sound macro-regulation. This will steadily strengthen the innovation capacity and competitiveness of China's economy.

Areas of focus in this regard include:

• furthering supply-side structural reform;

• making China a country of innovators;

• pursuing a rural revitalization strategy;

• implementing the coordinated regional development strategy;

• accelerating efforts to improve the socialist market economy; and

• making new ground in pursuing opening up on all fronts.

In a word, efforts to develop a modernized economy should be guided by our new vision for development with a focus on quality and efficiency, so as to achieve more equitable and more sustainable development.

加快完善社会主义市场经济体制

社会主义市场经济体制是中国共产党在建设中国特色社会主义进程中的一个重大理论和实践创新。1992年，中共十四大正式确立“我国经济体制改革的目标是建立社会主义市场经济体制”。经过20多年实践，中国社会主义市场经济体制已经初步建立，但仍存在不少问题，包括市场秩序不规范、生产要素市场发展滞后、市场规则不统一、市场竞争不充分等。

中共十九大报告作出加快完善社会主义市场经济体制的新要求。提出经济体制改革必须以完善产权制度和要素市场化配置为重点，实现产权有效激励、要素自由流动、价格反应灵活、竞争公平有序、企业优胜劣汰。要完善各类国有资产管理体制，改革国有资本授权经营体制，加快

Speeding Up the Improvement of the Socialist Market Economy

A socialist market economy is an innovative concept, and building such an economy represents an innovative undertaking by the CPC in its effort to build a socialist country with Chinese characteristics. The Party's 14th National Congress in 1992 decided that the goal of China's economic reform was to build a socialist market economy. Over the past 20 years, China's socialist market economy has taken shape, though some challenges persist, including weak regulation, stunted production factor market development, lack of regulatory consistency, and insufficient competition.

New measures were proposed in the report to the 19th CPC National Congress to accelerate improving our socialist market economy. Economic reform must focus on improving the system of property rights and strengthening the role of the market in allocating factors of production, to ensure that property rights provide effective incentives for individuals to engage in economic activities, and to ensure free flow of factors, market-based pricing, and fair and orderly competition, which determines the survival of businesses.

国有经济布局优化、结构调整、战略性重组，促进国有资产保值增值，推动国有资本做强做优做大，有效防止国有资产流失。深化国有企业改革，发展混合所有制经济，培育具有全球竞争力的世界一流企业。全面实施市场准入负面清单制度，清理废除妨碍统一市场和公平竞争的各种规定和做法，支持民营企业发展，激发各类市场主体活力。深化商事制度改革，打破行政性垄断，防止市场垄断，加快要素价格市场化改革，放宽服务业准入限制，完善市场监管体制。创新和完善宏观调控，发挥国家发展规划的战略导向作用，健全财政、货币、产业、区域等经济政策协调机制。完善促进消费的体制机制，增强消费对经济发展的基础性作用。深化投融资体制改革，发挥投资对优化供给结构的关键性作用。加快建立现代财政制度，建立权责清晰、财力协调、区域均衡的中央和地方财政关系。建立全面规范透明、标准科学、约束有力的预算制度，全面实施

It is important to better manage different types of state assets. The existing authorization process for using state assets needs reform. Public sector structural reform and strategic readjustment should proceed at an accelerated pace. Necessary measures should be taken to protect and increase the value of state assets, put them to effective use, and prevent asset loss.

State-owned enterprises need further reform to embrace a mixed-ownership formula. Efforts will be on-going to turn Chinese enterprises into world-class, globally competitive firms. A negative list for market access will be introduced nationwide. Regulations and practices that impede the development of a unified market and fair competition will be reviewed and abolished. Specific measures will be rolled out to support the development of private businesses, and help inject new dynamism into the business sector.

Business reform will continue, to break any monopoly imposed through administrative means, and prevent any other form of monopoly from imposing itself through market means. The reform will include the introduction of market-based mechanisms for factor pricing, relaxation of control over market access in the service sector, and plans to improve market regulation. It is essential to improve macroeconomic control in an innovative manner to enable national development plans to provide strategic guidance for economic activities, and to better coordinate

绩效管理。深化税收制度改革，健全地方税体系。深化金融体制改革，增强金融服务实体经济能力，提高直接融资比重，促进多层次资本市场健康发展。健全货币政策和宏观审慎政策双支柱调控框架，深化利率和汇率市场化改革。健全金融监管体系，守住不发生系统性金融风险的底线。

fiscal, monetary, industrial, regional, and other economic policies.

Measures will be taken to stimulate consumer spending, and strengthen the role of consumption in promoting economic growth. Further financial system reform is necessary, so as to enable investment services to play a crucial role in improving the supply-side structure.

A modern public finance system will be established, with clearly defined powers and responsibilities at the central and local levels, to ensure better fiscal coordination and greater balance between regions.

A comprehensive, transparent budgeting system will be in place with clearly defined, evidence-based and binding rules. Results-oriented performance appraisal will be introduced nationwide.

Further tax reform will continue, and local tax systems will be improved. Institutional reform in the financial sector is on-going, with the aim of making it better serve the real economy. Other reform objectives include increasing the proportion of direct financing, and promoting healthy development of a multilevel capital market.

We will further improve our two-pronged framework of monetary policy and macro-prudential regulation, and facilitate a move toward more market-based interest rate and exchange rate regimes. The bottom line is to improve the financial regulatory system to forestall systemic financial risks.

深化供给侧结构性改革

2015年11月10日，在中央财经领导小组第十一次会议上，习近平提出推进“供给侧改革”这一重要战略决策。当前和今后一个时期，中国经济发展面临的问题，供给和需求两侧都有，但矛盾的主要方面在供给侧。供给侧结构性改革，最终目的是满足需求，主攻方向是提高供给质量，根本途径是深化改革。最终目的是满足需求，就是要深入研究市场变化，理解现实需求和潜在需求，在解放和发展社会生产力中更好满足人民日益增长的物质文化需要。主攻方向是提高供给质量，就是要减少无效供给、扩大有效供给，着力提升整个供给体系质量，提高供给结构对需求结构的适应性。根本途径是深化改革，就是要完善市场在资源配置中起决定性作用的体制机制，深化行政管理体制改革，打破垄断，健全要素市场，使价格机制真正引导资源配置。当前供给侧结构性改革的主要任务是去产能、去库存、去杠杆、降成本、补短板。要通过一系列政策举措，特别是推动科技创新、发展实体经济、保障

Furthering Supply-Side Structural Reform

Xi Jinping emphasized the importance of "supply-side reform" at the 11th meeting of the CPC Central Leading Group for Financial and Economic Affairs on November 10, 2015. At present and for the foreseeable future, China will face a number of issues in its economic development in both supply and demand, but mostly on the supply side.

The ultimate goal of supply-side reform is to meet demand by improving quality through further reform. In order to meet demand, we must have a clear sense of market changes and understand the present and potential demand so that products can be made available through unleashed and increased productivity to meet the growing material and cultural needs of the population. In order to improve the quality of supply, we need to increase effective supply through a systemic improvement on the supply side so that ineffective supply is weeded out and supply is structured in a way that can effectively meet demand.

The fundamental approach to achieving this goal is in-depth reform. Institutions must be put in place to allow the market to play a decisive role in the allocation of resources. Further reform is also needed with the administrative management system in order to

和改善人民生活的政策措施，提高供给体系质量，为经济持续健康发展提供源源不断的内生动力。

break up monopoly and maintain a healthy factor market so that the price mechanism can truly serve as a guide for resource allocation. Structural reform on the supply side is designed to address overcapacity, reduce inventory, deleverage, lower costs, and tackle areas of weaknesses.

In order to resolve supply-side problems and generate constant driving forces for sustained and healthy economic growth, a number of policy measures are needed, especially those that aim to encourage innovation, growth in the real economy, and improved living standards.

加快建设创新型国家

创新是引领发展的第一动力，是建设现代化经济体系的战略支撑。党的十八大以来，中国在实施创新驱动发展战略上取得显著成就，科技进步对经济增长的贡献率从2012年的52.2%提高到2016年的56.2%，有力推动了产业转型升级。为了加快创新型国家建设，党的十九大报告强调，要瞄准世界科技前沿，强化基础研究，实现前瞻性基础研究、引领性原创成果重大突破。加强应用基础研究，拓展实施国家重大科技项目，突出关键共性技术、前沿引领技术、现代工程技术、颠覆性技术创新，为建设科技强国、质量强国、航天强国、网络强国、交通强国、数字中国、智慧社会提供有力支撑。加强国家创新体系建设，强化战略科技力量。深化科技体制改革，建立以企业为主体、市场为导向、产学研深度融合的技术创新体系，加强对中小企业创新的支持，促进科

Making China a Country of Innovators

Innovation is the primary driving force behind development; it is the strategic underpinning for building a modernized economy.

Since the 18th CPC National Congress, China has made remarkable progress in implementing its strategy for innovation-driven development, raising the contribution of science and technology to economic growth from 52.2 percent in 2012 to 56.2 percent in 2016, and boosting a structural shift and industrial upgrading.

The report to the 19th CPC National Congress emphasized that China should aim for the frontiers of science and technology, strengthen basic research, and make major breakthroughs in pioneering basic research and groundbreaking and original innovations. China will strengthen basic research in applied sciences, launch major national science and technology projects, and prioritize innovation in key generic technologies, cutting-edge frontier technologies, modern engineering technologies, and disruptive technologies. These efforts will provide powerful support for building China's strength in science and technology, product quality, aerospace, cyberspace, and transportation; and for building a digital China and a smart society.

China will improve its national innovation

技成果转化。倡导创新文化，强化知识产权创造、保护、运用。培养造就一大批具有国际水平的战略科技人才、科技领军人才、青年科技人才和高水平创新团队。

system and boost its strategic scientific and technological strength. It will further reform the management system for science and technology, and develop a market-oriented system for technological innovation in which enterprises are the main players and synergy is created through the joint efforts of enterprises, universities, and research institutes. It will support innovation by small and medium-sized enterprises and encourage the application of advances in science and technology.

China will foster a culture of innovation, and strengthen the creation, protection, and application of intellectual property. It should cultivate a large number of world-class scientists and technologists in strategically important fields, scientific and technological leaders, and young scientists and engineers, as well as high-performing innovation teams.

京津冀协同发展

推动京津冀协同发展是中国的一个重大国家战略，其核心是有序疏解北京非首都功能，调整经济结构和空间结构，走出一条内涵集约发展的新路子，探索出一种人口经济密集地区优化开发的模式，促进区域协调发展，形成新增长极。京津冀协同发展的范围包括北京市、天津市以及河北省的保定等11个地级市，计划在交通一体化、生态环境保护、产业升级转移等三大重点领域率先取得突破。2015年4月，中共中央政治局审议通过了《京津冀协同发展规划纲要》，为推动京津冀协同发展提供了顶层设计。京津冀协同发展不仅仅是解决北京发展面临的矛盾和问题的需要，也不仅仅是解决天津、河北发展面临的矛盾和问题的需要，而且是优化国家发展区

Coordinated Development of Beijing-Tianjin-Hebei Region

The Coordinated Development of Beijing-Tianjin-Hebei Region, as part of China's development strategy, aims at an orderly relocation of all non-essential functions from Beijing, the national capital, to neighboring locations. The move entails adjusting the economic structure and rationalizing space utilization, while exploring a new model of optimized coordinated development in a region with a dense population, to create a new growth pole in the region.

The broad region covers Beijing, Tianjin and 11 prefectural cities in the neighboring Hebei Province. Environmental protection, integrated transport services, and industrial upgrading and relocation are the three main areas of focus. In April 2015, the Political Bureau of the CPC Central Committee approved the Guidelines for the Coordinated Development of Beijing-Tianjin-Hebei Region as a top-level design for the development in this region in a coordinated manner.

Such a national strategy on coordinated development is needed in this region in order to resolve issues that have occurred in the development process in Beijing and the difficulties that Tianjin and Hebei have encountered in their own development. It is

域布局、优化社会生产力空间结构、打造新的经济增长极、形成新的经济发展方式的需要，是一个重大国家战略。

also needed in order to implement optimized regional planning for national development and a well mapped-out geographical distribution of production capacity.

长江经济带

2016年3月25日，中共中央政治局召开会议，审议通过了《长江经济带发展规划纲要》。发展长江经济带的导向是“共抓大保护、不搞大开发”。长江经济带涉及11个省市，即上海、江苏、浙江、安徽、江西、湖北、湖南、重庆、四川、云南和贵州。推动长江经济带发展的目标是：到2020年，生态环境明显改善，水资源得到有效保护和合理利用；长江黄金水道瓶颈制约有效疏畅、功能显著提升；创新驱动取得重大进展，培育形成一批世界级的企业和产业集群，参与国际竞争的能力显著增强；基本形成陆海统筹、双向开放，与“一带一路”建设深度融合的全方位对外开放新格局；发展的统筹度和整体性、协调性、可持续性进一步增强；重点领域和关键环节改革取得重要进展，协调统一、运行高效的长江流域管理体制全面建立，统一开放的现代市场体系基本建立；经济发展质量和效益大幅提升，基本形成引领全国经济社会发展的战略支撑带。到2030年，水环境和水生态质量全面改善，生态系统功能显著增强，水脉畅通、功能完备

The Yangtze Economic Belt

At its meeting on March 25, 2016, the Political Bureau of the CPC Central Committee approved the Guidelines for Development Along the Yangtze Economic Belt, which covers 11 provinces and municipalities – Shanghai, Jiangsu, Zhejiang, Anhui, Jiangxi, Hubei, Hunan, Chongqing, Sichuan, Yunnan and Guizhou. The Guidelines set the following goals to be achieved by 2020:

• marked improvement in environment, with effective protection and proper use of water resources;

• more efficient utilization of the Yangtze River waterway, with major constraints removed and transportation capacity enhanced;

• significant progress in innovation-driven growth as a large number of world-class businesses and industrial clusters take shape, with enhanced capability to compete in international markets;

• greater openness to the outside world on all fronts, with overall planning for regional and marine economic activities, emphasis on both domestic and international markets, and close integration with efforts in the Belt and Road Initiative;

• greater coordination and sustainability, with development activities in different areas

的长江全流域黄金水道全面建成，创新型现代产业体系全面建立，上中下游一体化发展格局全面形成，生态环境更加美好、经济发展更具活力、人民生活更加殷实，在全国经济社会发展中发挥更加重要的示范引领和战略支撑作用。

well-planned and properly implemented;

• significant progress in reform in key areas, with a well-coordinated and efficient management system and an open and unified market for the Yangtze River basin; and

• considerable qualitative improvement in economic development, with an initial capacity established that will allow the region to provide important support to national economic and social development.

In addition, the Guidelines also set the goals for 2030:

• overall improvement in the quality of water environment and the aquatic ecosystem;

• markedly enhanced ecological functions;

• completion of the development of the Yangtze River with navigable rivers and waterways;

• an innovation-intensive industrial system;

• integrated development in the upper, middle and lower reaches of the Yangtze River;

• a better environment and dynamic economic activities;

• higher living standards; and

• a stronger position for the region to play a role of pilot and provide important support to national economic and social development.

雄安新区

雄安新区是中共中央、国务院于2017年4月1日正式批准设立的国家级新区，涉及河北省雄县、容城、安新三县及周边部分区域。雄安新区，是以习近平同志为核心的党中央作出的一项重大的历史性战略选择，是继深圳经济特区和上海浦东新区之后又一具有全国意义的新区，是千年大计、国家大事。雄安新区建设将突出七个方面的重点任务：一是建设绿色智慧新城，建成国际一流、绿色、现代、智慧城市。二是打造优美生态环境，构建蓝绿交织、清新明亮、水城共融的生态城市。三是发展高端高新产业，积极吸纳和集聚创新要素资源，培育新动能。四是提供优质公共服务，建设优质公共设施，创建城市管理新样板。五是构建快捷高效交通网，打造绿色交通体系。六是推进体制机制改革，发挥市场在资源配置中的决定性作用和更好发挥政府作用，激发市场活力。七是扩大全方位对外开放，打造扩大开放新高地和对外合作新平台。雄安新区的设立，对于集中疏解北京非首都功能，探索人口经济密集地区优化开发新模式，调整

The Xiong'an New Area

The Xiong'an New Area is a national-level development zone established on April 1, 2017, by a decision of the CPC Central Committee and the State Council. The New Area includes Xiongxian County, Rongcheng County and Anxin County in Hebei Province, and some areas adjacent to the three counties. The decision is one of historic significance, which puts Xiong'an alongside Shenzhen Special Economic Zone and Shanghai Pudong New District as the third new district with nationwide influence. It is an important event for the nation and a grand plan for the long-term development of the country. Emphasis will be placed on the following seven areas as the New Area is being built:

• to build a green, modern and smart world-class city;

• to build an eco-friendly city with lush landscape with grass, trees and water;

• to develop high-end and high-tech industries with all the necessary inputs and resources for innovation to create new growth drivers;

• to provide high-quality public services and build excellent city facilities to create a new model for urban management;

• to build a green public transit system with rapid and efficient transportation;

• to promote structural and institutional

优化京津冀城市布局和空间结构，培育创新驱动发展新引擎，具有重大现实意义和深远历史意义。

reforms that will allow the market to play a decisive role in the allocation of resources and for the government to play its role as a catalyst to market activities; and

• to open up to the outside world on all fronts, with expanded areas of openness and new initiatives for cooperation with other countries.

Establishing the Xiong'an New Area is a move of immediate and far-reaching significance as it will help relocate non-essential functions from Beijing, the nation's capital, to neighboring locations, and explore a new model of optimized and coordinated development in a region with a dense population. It will help adjust the economic structure and rationalize space utilization to create a new engine for innovation-driven development.

推动形成全面开放新格局

开放带来进步，封闭必然落后。中共十九大报告强调，中国开放的大门不会关闭，只会越开越大，要推动形成全面开放新格局。推动形成全面开放新格局，就要以“一带一路”建设为重点，坚持引进来和走出去并重，遵循共商共建共享原则，加强创新能力开放合作，形成陆海内外联动、东西双向互济的开放格局。拓展对外贸易，培育贸易新业态新模式，推进贸易强国建设。实行高水平的贸易和投资自由化便利化政策，全面实行准入前国民待遇加负面清单管理制度，大幅度放宽市场准入，扩大服务业对外开放，保护外商投资合法权益。凡是在我国境内注册的企业，都要一视同仁、平等对待。优化区域开放布局，加大西部开放力度。赋予自由贸易

Making New Ground in Pursuing Opening Up on All Fronts

Openness brings progress, while self-seclusion leaves one behind. The report to the 19th CPC National Congress emphasized that China will not close its door to the world; it will only become more and more open.

China should pursue the Belt and Road Initiative as a priority, give equal emphasis to "bringing in" and "going global," follow the principle of achieving shared growth through discussion and collaboration, and increase openness and cooperation in building innovation capacity. With these efforts, we hope to make new ground in opening China further through links running eastward and westward, across land and over seas.

China will expand foreign trade, develop new models and new forms of trade, and turn it into a trader of quality. It will adopt policies to promote high-standard liberalization and facilitation of trade and investment; it will implement the system of preestablishment national treatment plus a negative list across the board, significantly ease market access, further open the service sector, and protect the legitimate rights and interests of foreign investors. All businesses registered in China will be treated equally.

China will improve the balance in

试验区更大改革自主权，探索建设自由贸易港。创新对外投资方式，促进国际产能合作，形成面向全球的贸易、投融资、生产、服务网络，加快培育国际经济合作和竞争新优势。

opening its different regions, and open the western region wider. It will grant more powers to pilot free trade zones to conduct reform, and explore the opening of free trade ports. It will develop new ways of making outbound investments, promote international cooperation on production capacity, form globally-oriented networks of trade, investment and financing, production, and services, and build up its strengths for international economic cooperation and competition.

健全人民当家做主制度体系，发展社会主义民主政治

Improving the System of Institutions Through Which the People Run the Country and Developing Socialist Democracy

社会主义民主政治

中国是工人阶级领导的、以工农联盟为基础的人民民主专政的社会主义国家，国家一切权力属于人民。中国社会主义民主是维护人民根本利益的最广泛、最真实、最管用的民主。发展社会主义民主政治就是要体现人民意志、保障人民权益、激发人民创造活力，用制度体系保证人民当家做主。

要长期坚持、不断发展我国社会主义民主政治，积极稳妥推进政治体制改革，推进社会主义民主政治制度化、规范化、法治化、程序化，保证人民依法通过各种途径和形式管理国家事务，管理经济文化事业，管理社会事务，巩固和发展生动活泼、安定团结的政治局面。

中国特色社会主义政治制度是中国共产党和中国人民的伟大创造。中国共产党人完全有信心、有能力把中国社会主义

Developing Socialist Democracy

China is a socialist country of people's democratic dictatorship under the leadership of the working class based on an alliance of workers and farmers; it is a country where all power of the state belongs to the people. China's socialist democracy is the broadest, most genuine, and most effective democracy to safeguard the fundamental interests of the people. The very purpose of developing socialist democracy is to give full expression to the will of the people, protect their rights and interests, spark their creativity, and provide systemic and institutional guarantees to ensure that the people run the country.

The pursuit of socialist democracy is a long-lasting, ever-evolving process. The political system reform must proceed steadily, to improve the institutional framework, norms, and procedures of socialist democracy, promote the rule of law, ensure effective participation of the people in accordance with the law through various channels in state affairs and in economic, cultural, and social governance, create a dynamic society, and enhance political stability and unity.

The political system of socialism with Chinese characteristics is a great invention of the CPC and the Chinese people. The Chinese Communists have every confidence

民主政治的优势和特点充分发挥出来，为人类政治文明进步作出充满中国智慧的贡献!

in the strengths and distinctive advantages of China's socialist democracy, and are able and willing to achieve its full potential so as to contribute to the political progress of mankind.

中国特色社会主义政治发展道路

中国特色社会主义政治发展道路，是近代以来中国人民长期奋斗历史逻辑、理论逻辑、实践逻辑的必然结果，是坚持党的本质属性、践行党的根本宗旨的必然要求。世界上没有完全相同的政治制度模式，政治制度不能脱离特定社会政治条件和历史文化传统来抽象评判，不能定于一尊，不能生搬硬套外国政治制度模式。其关键是坚持党的领导、人民当家做主、依法治国有机统一，核心是坚持和完善人民代表大会制度、中国共产党领导的多党合作和政治协商制度、民族区域自治制度以及基层群众自治制度，目的是不断推进社会主义政治制度自我完善和发展。要长期坚持、不断发展我国社会主义民主政治，积极稳妥推进政治体制改革，推进社会主义民主政治制度化、规范化、法治化、程序化，保证人民依法通过各种途径和形式

Socialist Political Advancement with Chinese Characteristics

The path of socialist political advancement with Chinese characteristics is the logical outcome of the evolution of history, theory, and practice as the Chinese people have long engaged in struggles since the advent of modern times. It is a requisite for maintaining the very nature of the Party and fulfilling its fundamental purpose.

No two political systems are entirely the same, and a political system cannot be judged in abstraction without regard for its social and political context, its history, and its cultural traditions. No one political system should be regarded as the only choice; and we should not just mechanically copy the political systems of other countries.

The key features of this process comprise Party leadership, the running of the country by the people, and law-based governance. It is informed by continued efforts to improve the system of people's congresses, multiparty cooperation and political consultation, regional ethnic autonomy, and community-level self-governance. Its objective is to steadily improve and develop the socialist political system.

We must make steady long-term efforts to strengthen China's socialist democracy,

管理国家事务，管理经济文化事业，管理社会事务，巩固和发展生动活泼、安定团结的政治局面。

and make active and prudent efforts to reform the political system and improve the institutions, standards, and procedures of socialist democracy. We should ensure that people participate, in accordance with the law and in various ways and forms, in the management of state, economic, cultural, and social affairs, and we should consolidate and enhance political stability, unity, and vitality.

中国特色社会主义法治道路

中国特色社会主义法治道路，就是在中国共产党领导下，紧紧围绕坚持和完善中国特色社会主义制度，深入贯彻中国特色社会主义法治理论，建设中国特色社会主义法治体系，坚持人民主体地位，坚持法律面前人人平等，坚持依法治国和以德治国相结合，坚持从中国实际出发，建设科学立法、严格执法、公正司法、全民守法的社会主义法治国家。坚持走中国特色社会主义法治道路，是中国的社会主义制度所决定的，是中国共产党深刻总结社会主义法治建设正反两方面经验得出的根本结论。

The Path of Law-Based Governance Under Chinese Socialism

The path of law-based governance under Chinese socialism is one led by the CPC. It tightly focuses on, maintains, and refines the institutions of Chinese socialism, thoroughly implements the theories of such governance, and establishes a legal system for Chinese socialism. It upholds the centrality of the people and the concept that everyone is equal before the law; it requires the integration of rule of law and rule by virtue; it demands that a law-based socialist country be developed based on China's actual conditions – one where legislation is scientific, law enforcement is strict, the judiciary is impartial, and the people are law-abiding.

Continuing to take the path of law-based governance under Chinese socialism is necessitated by China's socialist system, and it is based on a fundamental conclusion reached by the CPC after in-depth review of both the positive and negative experience of establishing socialist law-based governance.

坚持党的领导、人民当家做主、依法治国有机统一

党的领导是人民当家做主和依法治国的根本保证，人民当家做主是社会主义民主政治的本质特征，依法治国是党领导人民治理国家的基本方式，三者统一于我国社会主义民主政治伟大实践。在中国政治生活中，党是居于领导地位的，加强党的集中统一领导，支持人大、政府、政协和法院、检察院依法依章程履行职能、开展工作、发挥作用，这两个方面是统一的。要改进党的领导方式和执政方式，保证党领导人民有效治理国家；扩大人民有序参与政治，保证人民依法实行民主选举、民主协商、民主决策、民主管理、民主监督；维护国家法制统一、尊严、权威，加强人权法治保障，保证人民依法享有广泛权利和自由。巩固基层政权，完善基层民主制度，保障人民知情权、参与权、表达权、监督权。健全依法决策机制，构建决策科学、执行坚决、监督有力的权力运行机

The Unity of Party Leadership, Running of the Country by the People, and Law-Based Governance

Party leadership is the fundamental guarantee for ensuring that the people run the country and governance in China is law-based; that the people run the country is an essential feature of socialist democracy; and law-based governance is the basic way for the Party to lead the people in governing the country. These three elements are integral components of socialist democracy.

In China's political life, our Party exercises leadership. Strengthening the centralized, unified leadership of the Party on the one hand and, on the other, supporting the people's congresses, governments, committees of the Chinese People's Political Consultative Conference (CPPCC), courts, and procuratorates in performing their functions and playing their roles in accordance with the law and their charters, form a unified pair.

We will improve the way the Party exercises leadership and governance to ensure that it leads the people in effectively governing the country. We will expand the people's orderly political participation to see

制。各级领导干部要增强民主意识，发扬民主作风，接受人民监督，当好人民公仆。

that in accordance with law they engage in democratic elections, consultations, decision-making, management, and oversight. We should uphold the unity, sanctity, and authority of China's legal system, and strengthen legal protection for human rights to ensure that the people enjoy extensive rights and freedoms as prescribed by law. We should both consolidate government and improve the institutions of democracy at the primary level to ensure the people's rights to be informed, to participate, to be heard, and to oversee.

We will improve mechanisms for law-based decision-making, and put in place mechanisms for the exercise of power that ensure sound decision-making, resolute execution, and effective oversight. Officials at all levels must have a deeper understanding of democracy, be democratic in their conduct, willingly accept public oversight, and perform as they should in their role as public servants.

加强人民当家做主制度保障

社会主义民主政治的本质是人民当家做主。十九大报告强调，人民代表大会制度是坚持党的领导、人民当家做主、依法治国有机统一的根本政治制度安排，必须长期坚持、不断完善。要支持和保证人民通过人民代表大会行使国家权力。发挥人大及其常委会在立法工作中的主导作用，健全人大组织制度和工作制度，支持和保证人大依法行使立法权、监督权、决定权、任免权，更好发挥人大代表作用，使各级人大及其常委会成为全面担负起宪法法律赋予的各项职责的工作机关，成为同人民群众保持密切联系的代表机关。完善

Strengthening Institutional Guarantees to Ensure That the People Run the Country

The nature of socialist democracy is embodied in the role of the people in running the country. The report to the 19th CPC National Congress emphasized the imperative to continue to uphold and improve the system of people's congresses, a fundamental institutional framework that ensures the leadership by the Party, the running of the country by the people, and the rule of law. We should support and ensure the people's exercise of state power through people's congresses.

We should see to it that people's congresses and their standing committees play the leading role in lawmaking, and improve the organizational and working systems of people's congresses to support and ensure the exercise of their statutory powers of enacting laws, conducting oversight, making decisions, and appointing and removing officials. We should give better play to the role of deputies to people's congresses, and enable people's congresses at all levels and their standing committees to fully perform their functions as stipulated in the Constitution and the law, and to truly represent the people and maintain close ties with them. We should

人大专门委员会设置，优化人大常委会和专门委员会组成人员结构。

improve the setup of special committees of people's congresses and the composition of their standing committees and special committees.

党内民主

党内民主是指在中国共产党党内生活中，党员根据党章和党的其他规定，在平等的基础上，按照有关程序和形式，对党的事务参与、决策与管理。党内民主包括民主选举、民主决策、民主管理、民主监督，党内民主制度包括党的代表大会制度、集体领导制度、党内选举制度、维护党员民主权利制度、党内监督制度等形式。党内民主是由党的性质、党的宗旨和党的世界观决定的。中国共产党是执政党，党内民主的状况很大程度上决定着整个社会民主乃至人民民主的状况，党内政治生活的状况很大程度上决定着社会政治生活乃至国家政治生活的状况。2016年11月党的十八届六中全会审议通过的《关于新形势下党内政治生活的若干准则》指出：党内民主是党的生命，是党内政治生活积极健康的重要基础；保障党员民主权利，落实党员的知情权、参与权、选举权和监督权；党内决策、执行、监督等工作必须执行党章党规确定的民主原则和程序，任何党组织和个人都不得压制党内民主、破坏党内民主。习近平总书记要求，中央政治局带头发扬党内民主，积极营造民主讨

Intra-Party Democracy

Intra-Party democracy involves CPC members participating in the decision making and management of Party affairs on an equal footing and in accordance with the Constitution of the CPC and other Party regulations. Intra-Party democracy is exercised through democratic election, decision making, management and supervision. This is guaranteed by the systems of Party congress, collective leadership, intra-Party election, intra-Party supervision, and the system that protects Party members' democratic rights.

Intra-Party democracy is determined by the nature, mission and world view of the CPC. The CPC is the ruling party in China; the exercise of democracy overall in society is influenced to a large extent by how the CPC ensures intra-Party democracy, and intra-Party political activities to a large extent influence the political activities of the whole country.

The 18th Central Committee of the CPC deliberated over and approved the Code of Conduct for Intra-Party Political Life under New Circumstances at its sixth plenary session in November 2016. The Code of Conduct stipulates that democracy in the Party is the lifeline of the Party and provides an important foundation for active and healthy intra-Party political activity; that the democratic rights of Party members must be

论的良好氛围，鼓励讲真话、讲实话、讲心里话，善于运用民主的办法科学决策、协调关系、化解矛盾、推动工作。

guaranteed, and their rights to be informed, to participate, to vote, and to oversee Party affairs must be ensured; and that the democratic principles and procedures laid out in the Constitution and other regulations of the Party must be followed regarding intra-Party decision making and execution, supervision, and other work of the Party. No Party organization or individual shall be permitted to suppress or undermine democracy in the Party.

General Secretary Xi Jinping requires that the Political Bureau of the CPC Central Committee must take the lead in exercising intra-Party democracy, creating a positive environment for democratic discussion, encouraging people to tell the truth and speak to their mind, and be adept at taking democratic approaches to making decisions, coordinating various relations, solving problems, and making progress in relevant work.

社会主义协商民主

有事好商量，众人的事情由众人商量，是人民民主的真谛。协商民主是实现中国共产党的领导的重要方式，是中国社会主义民主政治的特有形式和独特优势，符合中国的现实国情，契合中国的政治文化传统。它不仅关注最终的决策结果，也关注决策过程中的广泛参与，不仅强调对多数人意见的尊重，也强调少数人意见的充分表达和权利的维护，拓宽了民主的广度，从而在最大程度上实现人民民主。人民政协是具有中国特色的制度安排，是社会主义协商民主的重要渠道和专门协商机构。中国将不断推进协商民主广泛多层制度化发展，深入开展立法协商、行政协商、民主协商、参政协商、社会协商。

Socialist Consultative Democracy

The essence of the people's democracy is that the people get to discuss their own affairs. Consultative democracy is an important way of effecting Party leadership and a model and strength unique to China's socialist democracy. It is rooted in China's realities and its political and cultural traditions, and embodies the distinctive strengths and advantages of China's socialist democracy. It focuses not only on outcomes of decision-making but also on broad participation in this process. It emphasizes not only the importance of respecting the opinions of the majority, but also the need to ensure that minority voices are heard. It broadens the scope of democracy, so that people can enjoy democracy to the greatest extent possible.

As a distinctively Chinese political institution, the CPPCC is a major channel for socialist consultative democracy, and its committees are special consultative bodies. China will continue to develop an extensive, multi-level institutional framework for consultative democracy informed by wide-ranging deliberations on legislation, government programs, issues related to democracy, state affairs, and social issues.

建设社会主义法治国家

2014年10月召开的中共十八届四中全会指出："全面推进依法治国，总目标是建设中国特色社会主义法治体系，建设社会主义法治国家。"中国特色社会主义法治体系由五个子系统构成：一是完备的法律规范体系，坚持以科学立法、民主立法、道德立法为衡量标准；二是高效的法治实施体系，以完善立法程序、完善司法制度、完善执政方式等为基本内容；三是严密的法治监督体系，包括全国人大的制约监督、行政机关的制约监督、司法机关的制约监督、社会舆论的制约监督、公民的制约监督等各类监督；四是有力的法治保障体系，以树立和维护司法权威、实施和促进司法公开、适应和满足法治需求等为重要保障；五是完善的党内法规体系。社会主义法治国家基本要求主要表现在法律完备而良好、法律权威、法律有效实施等方面。中国建设社会主义法治国家，必须走中国特色社会主义法治道路，坚持中国

Establishing a Socialist Law-Based Country

At its fourth plenary session in October 2014, the 18th CPC Central Committee noted that, "The overall goal of comprehensively promoting law-based governance is to develop a legal system with Chinese socialist characteristics, and to establish a socialist law-based country." Such a legal system is composed of five subsystems:

• a complete system of legal norms, to be assessed on whether the related legislation is scientific, democratic and ethical;

• a highly effective implementation system, the basic elements of which include a complete legislative system, a complete judicial system and a complete executive system;

• a rigorous system of legal oversight, including constraints and supervision by the National People's Congress, administrative agencies, judicial agencies, mass media and the general public;

• a powerful system of strong legal protections, including important protections for establishing and upholding judicial powers, implementing and promoting openness in judicial proceedings, and adapting to and satisfying the needs of law-based governance; and

• refined internal rules of the CPC.

The basic requirements of a socialist law-based country include a sound and

共产党的领导，坚持人民主体地位，坚持法律面前人人平等，坚持依法治国和以德治国相结合，坚持从中国实际出发。

complete set of laws, the authoritativeness of those laws and their effective implementation. If China is to establish a socialist law-based country, it must take the path of law-based governance under Chinese socialism, it must maintain the leadership of the CPC, and uphold the mastery of the people and the concept that everyone is equal before the law, and it must require the integration of rule of law and rule by virtue and demand that this be based on China's actual conditions.

深化机构和行政体制改革

改革开放以来，中国进行了多轮行政体制改革，受到民众广泛欢迎。党的十九大报告中提出了深化机构和行政体制改革的要求。主要举措包括：统筹考虑各类机构设置，科学配置党政部门及内设机构权力、明确职责。统筹使用各类编制资源，形成科学合理的管理体制，完善国家机构组织法。转变政府职能，深化简政放权，创新监管方式，增强政府公信力和执行力，建设人民满意的服务型政府。赋予省级及以下政府更多自主权。在省市县对职能相近的党政机关探索合并设立或合署办公。深化事业单位改革，强化公益属性，推进政事分开、事企分开、管办分离。这

In-depth Reform of Government Institutions and the System of Government Administration

Since the policy of reform and opening up was initiated, several rounds of institutional reform have been launched amid broad public support. Further refrom measures were proposed in the report to the 19th CPC National Congress, including an integrated approach to reconfurating the structures of Party and government institutions, and rational assignment of clearly defined responsibilities among these institutions and their internal bodies. There should be better coordination in the use of various types of staffing resources. Efforts will be made to rationalize the governance structure, and improve the organic law for state institutions.

Transformation of government functions will be accompanied by moves to further streamline government and delegate powers, improve regulatory practices, and strengthen government credibility and effectiveness, with the aim of building a service-oriented government able to satisfy the needs of the people.

More power should be delegated to governments at and below the provincial level, and possibilities will be explored to merge or

些举措被认为是适应国家治理体系现代化的重要内容，有利于进一步优化前期改革成果、提高行政效率、降低行政成本。

co-locate Party and government bodies with similar functions at the provincial, prefectural, and county levels. Reform of public institutions will continue, so as to ensure that they focus on serving the public good, without venturing into business activities, or being burdened with government functions. While government supervision remains indispensable, these institutions are responsible for their day-to-day operations.

These measures are critical to modernizing our national governance system, and will help build on the reform outcomes achieved to date to improve governance efficiency and reduce government costs.

巩固和发展爱国统一战线

统一战线是党的事业取得胜利的重要法宝，必须长期坚持。中共十九大报告提出巩固和发展爱国统一战线的要求。具体举措包括：要高举爱国主义、社会主义旗帜，牢牢把握大团结大联合的主题，坚持一致性和多样性统一，找到最大公约数，画出最大同心圆。坚持长期共存、互相监督、肝胆相照、荣辱与共，支持民主党派按照中国特色社会主义参政党要求更好履行职能。深化民族团结进步教育，铸牢中华民族共同体意识，加强各民族交往交流交融，促进各民族像石榴籽一样紧紧抱在一起，共同团结奋斗、共同繁荣发展。全面贯彻党的宗教工作基本方针，坚持我国宗教的中国化方向，积极引导宗教与社会主义社会相适应。加强党外知识分子工作，做好新的社会阶层人士工作，发挥他们在中国特色社会主义事业中的重要作用。构建亲清新型政商关系，促进非公

Consolidating and Developing the Patriotic United Front

The united front is an important way to ensure the success of the Party's cause, and we must maintain commitment to it long term.

The report to the 19th CPC National Congress highlighted the guidelines for consolidating and developing the Patriotic United Front. We must uphold the banner of patriotism and socialism, strive to achieve great unity and solidarity, balance commonality and diversity, and expand common ground and the convergence of interests. In handling its relationships with other Chinese political parties, the Communist Party of China is guided by the principles of long-term coexistence, mutual oversight, sincerity, and sharing the rough times and the smooth, and it supports these parties in performing their duties in accordance with the requirements of the Chinese socialist system for their participation in governance.

We will fully implement the Party's policies concerning ethnic groups, heighten public awareness of ethnic unity and progress, and create a strong sense of community for the Chinese nation. We will encourage more exchanges and interactions among different ethnic groups, helping them remain closely united like the seeds of a pomegranate that

有制经济健康发展和非公有制经济人士健康成长。广泛团结联系海外侨胞和归侨侨眷，共同致力于中华民族伟大复兴。

stick together, and work jointly for common prosperity and development.

We will fully implement the Party's basic policy on religious affairs, uphold the principle that religions in China must be Chinese in orientation and provide active guidance to religions so that they can adapt themselves to socialist society. We will encourage intellectuals who are not Party members and people belonging to new social groups to play the important roles they have in building socialism with Chinese characteristics. We should form a new type of cordial and clean relationship between government and business, promote healthy growth of the non-public sector of the economy, and encourage those working in this sector to achieve success. We will maintain extensive contacts with overseas Chinese nationals, returned Chinese and their relatives and unite them so that they can join our endeavors to revitalize the Chinese nation.

中华民族共同体意识

中华民族共同体意识是习近平倡导的重要理念之一。2014年9月，他在中央民族工作会议暨国务院第六次全国民族团结进步表彰大会上提出，加强中华民族大团结，长远和根本的是增强文化认同，建设各民族共有精神家园，积极培养中华民族共同体意识。党的十九大报告进一步提出，铸牢中华民族共同体意识，加强各民族交往交流交融，促进各民族像石榴籽一样紧紧抱在一起，共同团结奋斗、共同繁荣发展。中华民族共同体就是一个由56个民族组成的，有共同认同的血缘融通、流动交汇有机体，是一个历经五千年风雨锻造而成的命运共同体、政治共同体、社会共同体、文化共同体。历史证明，中华民族共同体意识是国家统一之基、民族团结之本、精神力量之魂。实现中华民族伟大复兴的中国梦，需要进一步培育中华民族共同体意识，打牢各族人民团结奋斗的政治基础、思想基础和社会基础。

A Strong Sense of Community for the Chinese Nation

Xi Jinping advocates a strong sense of community for the Chinese nation. He pointed out, at the Central Conference on Ethnic Affairs in September 2014, that to consolidate the unity of the Chinese nation, an effective long-term approach is to foster shared cultural identity and cultural belonging, and create a strong sense of community for the Chinese nation.

Xi reiterated this view in his report to the 19th National Congress of the CPC and called for more exchanges and interactions among different ethnic groups so that they will unite closely and work together for common prosperity and development.

The Chinese nation is composed of 56 ethnic groups with close internal blood ties. It is a community with a shared history, culture, and political and social evolution dating back more than 5,000 years. History proves that a sense of community is the foundation for China's national unity and ethnic solidarity, and the soul of China. To make the Chinese Dream come true, China should further enhance public awareness of this sense, and cement the political, theoretical and social foundations for all ethnic groups to unite.

亲清新型政商关系

2016年3月4日，习近平看望出席全国政协十二届四次会议的民建、工商联委员并参加他们的小组讨论时，提出了“新型政商关系”的理念，并用“亲”和“清”两个字进行了概括。对领导干部而言，所谓“亲”，就是坦荡真诚同民营企业接触交往，特别是在民营企业遇到困难和问题情况下更要积极作为、靠前服务，对非公有制经济人士多关注、多谈心、多引导，帮助解决实际困难，真心实意支持民营经济发展。所谓“清”，就是同民营企业家的关系要清白、纯洁，不能有贪心私心，不能以权谋私，不能搞权钱交易。对民营企业家而言，所谓“亲”，就是积极主动同各级党委和政府及部门多沟通多交流，讲真话，说实情，建诤言，满腔热情支持地方

A New Type of Government-Business Relationship

On March 4, 2016, Xi Jinping proposed a "new type of government-business relationship" when he met with members of the National Democratic Construction Association and the All-China Federation of Industry and Commerce in a discussion at the Fourth Session of the 12th CPPCC National Committee. He described it as a "close" and "clean" relationship.

In a "close" relationship, government officials must be open and forthright when interacting with private businesses, taking the initiative to provide them with the needed services and help them when they come across difficulties or problems. Government officials should spend more time communicating with private sector entrepreneurs, consulting with them, offering them the needed advice and helping them resolve issues in their operations, in a genuine effort to help grow the private sector.

For a "clean" relationship, government officials should keep a straightforward relationship with private businesses with no hidden agenda, or any intention or attempt to use their positions or authority for private interests or financial gains.

Private businesses, for their part, must

发展。所谓“清”，就是要洁身自好、走正道，做到遵纪守法办企业、光明正大搞经营。

maintain a "close" relationship with the government by being upfront and truthful about their situation, communicate with the CPC committees and government departments at different levels, and present candid views and constructive suggestions that will help promote local development.

A "clean" relationship means honest corporate citizens who do what is right and operate in full compliance with relevant laws and regulations.

国家监察体制改革

国家监察体制改革是中国正在进行的一项事关全局的重大政治体制改革举措。2016年11月，中国在北京市、山西省、浙江省开展国家监察体制改革试点，探索在上述三省市设立各级监察委员会。党的十九大报告提出，深化国家监察体制改革，将试点工作在全国推开，组建国家、省、市、县监察委员会，同党的纪律检查机关合署办公，实现对所有行使公权力的公职人员监察全覆盖。制定国家监察法，依法赋予监察委员会职责权限和调查手段，用留置取代"两规"措施。2017年10月，十二届全国人大常委会第三十次会议审议通过全国人大常委会关于在全国各地推开国家监察体制改革试点工作的决定草案。2017年底2018年初召开的省、市、县人民代表大会将全部产生监察委员会。

Reform of the National Supervision System

Reform of the national supervision system is an important, cross-cutting political institutional reform measure. Pilot reform projects were rolled out in November 2016 in Beijing, Shanxi, and Zhejiang to explore the feasibility of establishing supervisory commissions at the provincial and local levels.

We will further reform of the national supervision system, extend trial projects throughout the country, and establish supervisory commissions at the national, provincial, prefectural, and county levels, which work together with the Party's disciplinary inspection commissions as one office while keeping their own identity. This will ensure that supervision covers everyone working in the public sector who exercises public power. A national supervision law will be formulated. Supervisory commissions will be given responsibilities, powers, and means of investigation in accordance with law. The practice of *shuanggui* (A form of intraparty disciplinary action that requires a Party member under investigation to cooperate with questioning at a designated place and a designated time.) will be replaced by detention.

A draft decision on expanding pilot projects on reform of supervision system throughout the country was adopted in

监察体制改革与地方人大换届工作紧密衔接，将推动改革持续深入，实现全面从严治党与全面深化改革、全面依法治国有机统一。

October 2017 by the Standing Committee of the 12th National People's Congress at its 30th session. People's congresses at the provincial, municipal or county levels convened at the end of 2017 or at the beginning of 2018 are all set to establish supervisory commissions. Reform of supervision system will dovetail with elections of deputies to local people's congresses, and proceed as part of an integrated effort to enforce strict Party discipline, pursue in-depth reform, and promote the rule of law.

| 汉英对照 |

十九大篇

19th National Congress of the Communist Party of China

中国关键词

KEYWORDS TO UNDERSTAND CHINA

权 威 解 读 当 代 中 国

中国外文出版发行事业局（CIPG）
当代中国与世界研究院（ACCWS）
中国翻译研究院（CATL）

新世界出版社
NEW WORLD PRESS

CONTENTS
目 录

坚定文化自信，推动社会主义文化繁荣兴盛 · Building Stronger Cultural Confidence and Helping Socialist Culture to Flourish

提高保障和改善民生水平，加强和创新社会治理 · Growing Better at Ensuring and Improving People's Wellbeing and Strengthening and Developing New Approaches to Social Governance

加快生态文明体制改革，建设美丽中国 · Speeding Up Reform of the System for Developing an Ecological Civilization, and Building a Beautiful China

坚持走中国特色强军之路，全面推进国防和军队现代化 · Staying Committed to the Chinese Path of Building Strong Armed Forces and Fully Advancing the Modernization of National Defense and the Military

坚持"一国两制"，推进祖国统一 · Upholding "One Country, Two Systems" and Moving Toward National Reunification

坚持和平发展道路，推动构建人类命运共同体 · Following a Path of Peaceful Development and Working to Build a Community with a Shared Future for Humanity

坚定不移全面从严治党，不断提高党的执政能力和领导水平 · Exercising Strict Governance over the Party and Improving the Party's Ability to Govern and Lead

坚定文化自信，推动社会主义文化繁荣兴盛

Building Stronger Cultural Confidence and Helping Socialist Culture to Flourish

中国特色社会主义文化发展道路

2011年10月召开的中共十七届六中全会提出，坚持中国特色社会主义文化发展道路，努力建设社会主义文化强国。中国特色社会主义文化发展道路可以概括为：高举中国特色社会主义理论旗帜，坚持社会主义先进文化前进方向，把握科学发展这个主题，围绕建设社会主义核心价值体系这个任务，坚持以满足人民精神文化需求为出发点和落脚点，坚持以开放为取向，坚持以优秀传统文化为滋养，将改革创新作为发展动力。全会还深刻指出，“文化引领时代风气之先，是最需要创新的领域。要建设社会主义文化强国，动力和出路都在于改革和创新。”全会对中国特色社

Cultural Development Under Socialism with Chinese Characteristics

At its sixth plenary session held in October 2011, the 17th CPC Central Committee proposed a guideline for continued cultural development under socialism with Chinese characteristics in order to make China a socialist country with advanced culture. Such strategy for cultural development covers the following: China remains committed to theory of socialism with Chinese characteristics as it advances cultural development, with focus on the scientific approach to development and the core values of Chinese socialism, for the purpose of satisfying the intellectual and cultural needs of the people. There will be continued emphasis on opening up to the outside world and on traditional culture as a source of enrichment to this process, which is also to be driven by innovation.

It was also pointed out at the plenary session that "culture is an area that needs innovation the most as it defines the way in which a new era takes shape. Reform and innovation are therefore the driver and solution if we want to make China a socialist country with advanced culture." Following extensive deliberations, the plenary session provided us with the guideline and associated

会主义文化发展道路的科学论断，是我们要长期坚持的道路和方针。

principles for advancing cultural development under socialism with Chinese characteristics.

牢牢掌握意识形态工作领导权

意识形态决定文化的前进方向和发展道路。党的十九大报告强调，牢牢掌握意识形态工作领导权。具体举措包括：必须推进马克思主义中国化时代化大众化，建设具有强大凝聚力和引领力的社会主义意识形态，使全体人民在理想信念、价值理念、道德观念上紧紧团结在一起。要加强理论武装，推动新时代中国特色社会主义思想深入人心。深化马克思主义理论研究和建设，加快构建中国特色哲学社会科学，加强中国特色新型智库建设。高度重视传播手段建设和创新，提高新闻舆论传播力、引导力、影响力、公信力。加强互联网内容建设，建立网络综合治理体系，营造清朗的网络空间。落实意识形态工作责任制，加强阵地建设和管理，注意区分

Holding Firmly the Leading Position in Ideological Work

Ideology determines the direction a culture should take and the path it should follow as it develops. The 19th CPC National Congress emphasized that the Party should hold firmly the leading position in ideological work. We must continue to adapt Marxism to China's conditions, keep it up-to-date, and enhance its popular appeal. We will develop socialist ideology that has the ability to unite and the power to inspire the people to embrace shared ideals, convictions, values, and moral standards. We will better arm ourselves with theory and increase the public appeal of the Thought on Socialism with Chinese Characteristics for a New Era. We will work harder to study and develop Marxist theory, work faster to develop philosophy and social sciences with Chinese characteristics, and develop new types of think tanks with distinctive Chinese features.

We will maintain the right tone in public communication, give priority to improving means of communication and to creating new ones, and strengthen the penetration, guidance, influence, and credibility of the media. We will provide more and better online content and put in place a system for integrated internet management to ensure a clean

政治原则问题、思想认识问题、学术观点问题，旗帜鲜明反对和抵制各种错误观点。

cyberspace. We will implement the system of responsibility for ideological work, and further consolidate our positions and improve management in this field. We will distinguish between matters of political principle, issues of understanding and thinking, and academic viewpoints, but we must oppose and resist various erroneous views with a clear stand.

培育和践行社会主义核心价值观

2012年11月召开的中共十八大提出了培育和践行社会主义核心价值观的根本任务，强调要倡导富强、民主、文明、和谐，倡导自由、平等、公正、法治，倡导爱国、敬业、诚信、友善。社会主义核心价值观把涉及国家、社会、公民三个层面的价值要求融为一体，体现了社会主义意识形态的本质要求，体现了社会主义制度在思想和精神层面的质的规定性，是当代中国精神的集中体现，凝结着全体人民共同的价值追求。社会主义核心价值观深入回答了要建设什么样的国家、建设什么样的社会、培育什么样的公民的重大问题。培育和践行社会主义核心价值观，要以培养担当民族复兴大任的时代新人为着眼点，强化教育引导、实践养成、制度保障，把社会主义核心价值观融入社会发展各方面，转化为人们的情感认同和行为习惯。

Fostering Core Values of Socialism

The 18th CPC National Congress, held in November 2012, called for a major drive to foster the core values of Chinese socialism, as represented at three different levels for the state, for society, and for individual citizens. At the state level, China must be a country with prosperity, democracy, civility, and harmony. For society, it should be one of freedom, equality, justice and the rule of law. And for individual citizens, we need patriotism, professionalism, integrity and good will.

The core values of socialism, as an aggregation of these goals, are an essential part of the socialist ideology and define the ideological and intellectual pursuits of the socialist system. They embody the essence of advanced culture, and are the true expressions of the value pursued by the whole Chinese people.

In the core values of socialism, we have found answers to important questions: what kind of a country and society do we want to build, and what kind of citizenry do we need to develop? To develop and promote the core values of socialism, we must first start with education, to make sure that these values become part of our daily life and that they are rooted in the traditional culture in which we as Chinese take such great pride.

讲好中国故事

2013年8月，在全国宣传思想工作会议上，习近平提出了“讲好中国故事”的明确要求。他不仅是倡导者，也是践行者，尤其是在对外交往中，讲述了很多温暖人心的故事，拉近了中外民众的距离，向世界形象传递了中国观点和中国态度。这些故事贯穿着中国历史文化之“道”，中国改革发展之“道”，中国参与世界治理之“道”。实现中华民族伟大复兴的中国梦，是当代中国最宏大、最精彩的故事。中国故事能不能讲好，中国声音能不能传播好，关键要看受众是否愿意听、听得懂，能否形成良性互动，产生更多共鸣。为此，中国正在通过加强国际传播能力建设、推动传统媒体与新兴媒体融合发展、打造融通中外的话语体系等措施，展现真实、立体、全面的中国，提高国家文化软实力。

Telling China's Stories

At the National Publicity and Ideological Work Conference in August 2013, Xi Jinping indicated that we must do a better job of "telling China's stories." He is not only the advocate, but also the lead practitioner of this idea. As he interacts with people of other countries, President Xi effectively conveys to the outside world China's views and positions, telling stories that warm people's hearts and bring the Chinese people and people of other countries closer.

These stories tell how China's history and culture advance, how China has forged ahead with its reform and development, and how China is involved in global governance. The most exciting story in China today is the extensive efforts that the Chinese people are making to achieve the Chinese Dream of national rejuvenation. To tell China's stories and convey China's voice effectively, we must make sure that we tell stories that people want to hear and are able to understand, stories that they feel they want to respond to, and something that resonates with their own life. China is now making a greater effort to increase its international outreach by promoting the integrated development of traditional and emerging media and building up a discourse system that is capable of effective international communication.

提高保障和改善民生水平，加强和创新社会治理

Growing Better at Ensuring and Improving People's Wellbeing and Strengthening and Developing New Approaches to Social Governance

坚决打赢脱贫攻坚战

改革开放近40年来，中国经济社会发展取得很大成就，几亿贫困人口脱贫，完成这期间全世界超过70%的减贫任务。但由于中国还处在社会主义初级阶段，由于国家大、各地发展条件不同，中国还有为数不少的困难群众，扶贫开发依然任重道远。让贫困人口和贫困地区同全国一道进入全面小康社会是中国共产党的庄严承诺。要动员全党全国全社会力量，坚持精准扶贫、精准脱贫，坚持中央统筹省负总责市县抓落实的工作机制，强化党政一把手负总责的责任制，坚持大扶贫格局，注重扶贫同扶志、扶智相结合，深入实施东西部扶贫协作，重点攻克深度贫困地区脱贫任务，确保到2020年中国现行标准下农

Winning the Battle Against Poverty

Over the past 40 years since reform and opening up started, China has made great economic and social progress, lifting hundreds of millions of people out of poverty, accounting for over 70 percent of the global poverty reduction during the period. But China is still in the primary stage of socialism; different regions have different levels of development; and a sizable number of poor people persist. So the battle against poverty is far from over.

Seeing that poor people and poor areas will enter the moderately prosperous society together with the rest of the country is a solemn promise made by our Party. We should mobilize the energies of our whole Party, our whole country, and our whole society, and continue to implement targeted poverty reduction and alleviation measures. We will operate on the basis of a working mechanism whereby the central government makes overall plans, provincial-level governments take overall responsibility, and city and county governments ensure implementation; and we will strengthen the system for making heads of Party committees and governments at each level assume the overall responsibility for poverty alleviation.

Poverty alleviation is an all-encompassing

村贫困人口实现脱贫，贫困县全部摘帽，解决区域性整体贫困，做到脱真贫、真脱贫。

campaign. We will pay particular attention to helping people increase confidence in their own ability to lift themselves out of poverty and see that they can access the education they need to do so. We will strengthen collaboration on poverty alleviation between the eastern and western regions; and we will provide focused assistance to areas of extreme poverty. We must ensure that by the year 2020, all rural residents living below the current poverty line have been lifted out of poverty, and poverty is eliminated in all poor counties and regions. Poverty alleviation should reach those who truly need it and deliver genuine outcomes.

就业是最大的民生

中国是一个13亿多人口的发展中大国，庞大的人口基数决定了就业问题是中国最大的民生问题。党的十八大以来，在以习近平同志为核心的党中央的坚强领导下，各项促就业、助创业的政策出台，就业状况持续改善，成功解决了6500万人的就业问题。党的十九大报告明确提出，就业是最大的民生。要坚持就业优先战略和积极就业政策，实现更高质量和更充分就业。通过大规模开展职业技能培训，提供全方位公共就业服务，破除妨碍劳动力、人才社会性流动的体制机制弊端，使人人都有通过辛勤劳动实现自身发展的机会。

Employment, Pivotal to the People's Wellbeing

China is a large developing country with a population of over 1.3 billion. Because of its big population size, employment remains the biggest challenge China faces in its efforts to improve the people's wellbeing. Since the Party's 18th National Congress, a series of policies promoting job creation and entrepreneurship have been launched under the leadership of the Party Central Committee with Xi Jinping at its core, leading to a steady improvement in the overall jobs picture, with 65 million new jobs added.

The report to the 19th CPC National Congress highlighted the pivotal importance of employment to the wellbeing of the people. It called for more proactive measures to promote job creation, achieve fuller employment and create better jobs. These measures include expanding vocational skills training programs, providing extensive public employment services, and removing institutional barriers that block mobility of labor and talent to ensure that everyone has a chance for career success through hard work.

全面建成多层次社会保障体系

社会保障是民生的保护网、风险的缓冲器，与人民幸福安康息息相关，关系国家长治久安。党的十九大报告提出，按照兜底线、织密网、建机制的要求，全面建成覆盖全民、城乡统筹、权责清晰、保障适度、可持续的多层次社会保障体系。为实现此政策目标，中国将主要采取如下措施：全面实施全民参保计划；完善城镇职工基本养老保险和城乡居民基本养老保险制度，尽快实现养老保险全国统筹；完善统一的城乡居民基本医疗保险制度和大病保险制度；完善失业、工伤保险制度；建立全国统一的社会保险公共服务平台；统

Building a Multi-Tiered Social Security System

Social security provides a safety net for the people and a buffer against risk. It is vital to the wellbeing of the people and the long-term stability of our country.

The report to the 19th CPC National Congress called for measures to help those most in need, to build a strong safety net, and to create necessary mechanisms to implement a sustainable multi-tiered social security system, one that covers the entire population, addresses urban and rural issues in an integrated manner, clearly defines rights and responsibilities of beneficiaries and all other actors involved, and provides adequate levels of protection.

To this end, China will implement a universal health insurance plan, improve the basic pension schemes for urban employees and for rural and non-working urban residents, and take speedy action to incorporate all pension schemes into a unified national framework. Improvement is also called for of the unified systems of basic medical insurance and critical illness insurance for rural and non-working urban residents, as well as unemployment and work-related injury insurance. A unified national platform for social security public services will be established. An integrated system is necessary to provide

筹城乡社会救助体系，完善最低生活保障制度，完善社会救助、社会福利、慈善事业、优抚安置等制度。

social assistance in both urban and rural areas, and the basic needs of the people must be satisfied. In addition, we will improve our social welfare system, encourage charitable giving, and ensure that armed forces veterans and their family members receive special benefits and services.

实施健康中国战略

人民健康是民族昌盛和国家富强的重要标志。要完善国民健康政策，为人民群众提供全方位全周期健康服务。深化医药卫生体制改革，全面建立中国特色基本医疗卫生制度、医疗保障制度和优质高效的医疗卫生服务体系，健全现代医院管理制度。加强基层医疗卫生服务体系和全科医生队伍建设。全面取消以药养医，健全药品供应保障制度。坚持预防为主，深入开展爱国卫生运动，倡导健康文明生活方式，预防控制重大疾病。实施食品安全战略，让人民吃得放心。坚持中西医并重，传承发展中医药事业。支持社会办医，发展健康产业。促进生育政策和相关经济社会政策配套衔接，加强人口发展战略研究。积极应对人口老龄化，构建养老、孝

Carrying Out the Healthy China Initiative

A healthy population is a key mark of a prosperous nation and a strong country. We will improve the national health policy, and ensure the delivery of comprehensive lifecycle health services for our people. We will further reform of the medicine and health-care system, establish distinctively Chinese systems for providing basic healthcare, medical insurance, and quality and efficient healthcare services, and develop a sound modern hospital management system.

We will improve community-level health-care services, and strengthen the ranks of general practitioners. We will put an end to the practices of hospitals funding their operations with profits from overpriced drugs, and improve the system for medicine supply.

We will, with emphasis on prevention, carry out extensive patriotic health campaigns, promote healthy and positive lifestyles, and prevent and control major diseases. We will initiate a food safety strategy to ensure that people have peace of mind about what they're putting on their plates. We will support both traditional Chinese medicine and Western medicine, and ensure the preservation and development of traditional Chinese medicine. We will support the development of private hospitals and health-related industries.

老、敬老政策体系和社会环境，推进医养结合，加快老龄事业和产业发展。

We will work to ensure that our childbirth policy meshes with related economic and social policies, and carry out research on the population development strategy. As we respond proactively to population aging, we will adopt policies and foster a social environment in which senior citizens are respected, cared for, and live happily in their later years. We will provide integrated elderly care and medical services, and accelerate the development of old-age programs and industries.

打造共建共治共享的社会治理格局

2016年3月发布的《中华人民共和国国民经济和社会发展第十三个五年规划纲要》提出"构建全民共建共享的社会治理格局"，明确了社会治理不是简单的管理与被管理的关系，而是共同参与的理念。这是探索实现中国社会治理现代化的指导思想和实践路径。十九大报告进一步指出，加强社会治理制度建设，完善党委领导、政府负责、社会协同、公众参与、法治保障的社会治理体制，提高社会治理社会化、法治化、智能化、专业化水平。加强预防和化解社会矛盾机制建设，正确处理人民内部矛盾。树立安全发展理念，弘扬生命至上、安全第一的思想，健全公共安全体系，完善安全生产责任制，坚决遏制重特大安全事故，提升防灾减灾救灾能力。加快社会治安防控体系建设，依法打击和惩治黄赌毒黑拐骗等违法犯罪活动，保护人民人身权、财产权、人格权。加强

Establishing a Social Governance Model Based on Collaboration, Participation, and Common Interests

A proposal for promoting participatory social governance was unveiled in March 2016 in the 13th Five-year Plan for Economic and Social Development. It emphasizes the participatory nature of social governance, rejecting the notion that governance is about the relationship between the governing elite and the governed. It provides guiding principles for modernizing China's thinking on social governance and for implementing social governance initiatives.

The report to the 19th CPC National Congress highlighted the need to strengthen the institution building in social governance and improve the law-based social governance model under which Party committees exercise leadership, government assumes responsibility, non-governmental actors provide assistance, and the public get involved. We will strengthen public participation and rule of law in social governance, and make such governance smarter and more specialized.

We will improve mechanisms for preventing and defusing social tensions, and properly handle problems among the people.

社会心理服务体系建设，培育自尊自信、理性平和、积极向上的社会心态。加强社区治理体系建设，推动社会治理重心向基层下移，发挥社会组织作用，实现政府治理和社会调节、居民自治良性互动。

We will promote safe development, and raise public awareness that life matters most and that safety comes first; we will improve the public safety system and the responsibility system for workplace safety; we will take resolute measures to prevent serious and major accidents, and build up our capacity for disaster prevention, mitigation, and relief.

We will accelerate development of the crime prevention and control system, combat and punish in accordance with law all illegal and criminal activities such as pornography, gambling, drug abuse, gang violence, kidnapping, and fraud, and protect people's personal rights, property rights, and right to dignity. We will improve the system of public psychological services, and cultivate self-esteem, self-confidence, rationality, composure, and optimism among our people. We will strengthen the system for community governance, shift the focus of social governance to the community level, leverage the role of social organizations, and see that government's governance efforts on the one hand and society's self-regulation and residents' self-governance on the other reinforce each other.

加快生态文明体制改革，建设美丽中国

Speeding Up Reform of the System for Developing an Ecological Civilization, and Building a Beautiful China

建设美丽中国

建设生态文明，关系人民福祉，关乎民族未来。党的十八大报告提出，努力建设美丽中国，实现中华民族永续发展。党的十九大报告进一步提出，加快生态文明体制改革，建设美丽中国。建设美丽中国是中国梦的重要内容，就是要按照尊重自然、顺应自然、保护自然的理念，坚持“既要金山银山，又要绿水青山”“绿水青山就是金山银山”的理念，贯彻节约资源和保护环境的基本国策，更加自觉地推动绿色发展、循环发展、低碳发展。建设美丽中国，就是要给自然留下更多修复空间，给农业留下更多良田，为子孙后代留下天蓝、地绿、水清的生产生活环境。中国梦的实现不以牺牲环境为代价，在发展经济的同时，保护好生态环境。建设“美丽中国”，有利于中国的长远发展，也将助推世

Building a Beautiful China

A beautiful environment is beneficial to the people and the future of the nation. The report to the 18th National Congress of the CPC called for hard work to build a beautiful country, and achieve lasting and sustainable development of the Chinese nation. The report to the 19th CPC National Congress proposed speeding up reform of the system for developing an ecological civilization, and building a beautiful China.

Building a beautiful China is an important part of the Chinese Dream. It calls for respecting, protecting and being in harmony with nature, based on the understanding that "lucid waters and lush mountains are invaluable assets." China should implement its key national policy on resource conservation, environmental protection, and promotion of green, circular and low-carbon development. The initiative underscores the need to leave more space for nature to renew itself, to keep more land for cultivation, and to bequeath a better working and living environment to future generations so that they can be blessed with a blue sky, green fields, and clean water.

The Chinese Dream will not be realized at the expense of the environment. Economic development should be accompanied by strong measures to protect the environment.

界可持续发展，更有助于实现人类共同的梦想：保护美丽的地球。“美丽中国”的目标将在2035年基本实现。

Building a beautiful China will be of benefit to the country's long-term development, to promoting sustainable global development, and to fulfilling the universal dream of protecting our beautiful earth.

According to China's two-stage development plan, the basic elements of a beautiful China will be in place by 2035.

社会主义生态文明观

社会主义生态文明是继传统工业文明之后的一个崭新的文明形态，它是人类文明发展到一定阶段的必然产物。2012年11月，党的十八大作出“大力推进生态文明建设”的战略决策，把生态文明建设纳入中国特色社会主义“五位一体”总体布局并明确写入党章；2015年10月，党的十八届五中全会又将“绿色发展”作为五大发展理念之一。党的十九大报告进一步强调，建设生态文明是中华民族永续发展的千年大计。要坚持人与自然的和谐共生，转变经济发展方式，建设美丽中国。要牢固树立社会主义生态文明观，推动形成人与自然和谐发展现代化建设新格局，为保护生态环境作出我们这代人的努力。

A Socialist Approach to Environmental Protection

A socialist approach to environmental protection represents new thinking that has emerged in the wake of traditional industrial civilization. It is a logical outcome of the development of human civilization. The commitment to promote environmental protection was highlighted in November 2012 at the 18th CPC National Congress and incorporated in the Party Constitution, as one of the five areas of the Five-sphere Integrated Plan, which also emphasizes economic, political, cultural and social development. At its fifth plenary session in October 2015, the 18th CPC Central Committee also underscored the need for green development as one of the Five Concepts for Development.

The report to the 19th CPC National Congress reaffirmed the vital importance of environmental protection to the survival of our nation, and the imperative to transform our economic development model and to build a beautiful China. A socialist approach to environmental protection is essential to maintaining harmony between man and nature as we pursue modernization and to fulfilling our generation's responsibility to the natural environment.

推进绿色发展

作为"五大发展理念"之一，绿色发展注重的是解决人与自然和谐相处的问题。十九大报告指出，加快建立绿色生产和消费的法律制度和政策导向，建立健全绿色低碳循环发展的经济体系。构建市场导向的绿色技术创新体系，发展绿色金融，壮大节能环保产业、清洁生产产业、清洁能源产业。推进能源生产和消费革命，构建清洁低碳、安全高效的能源体系。推进资源全面节约和循环利用，实施国家节水行动，降低能耗、物耗，实现生产系统和生活系统循环链接。倡导简约适度、绿色低碳的生活方式，反对奢侈浪费和不合理消费，开展创建节约型机关、绿

Green Development

One of the Five Concepts for Development, green development highlights the importance of harmony between man and nature.

The report to the 19th CPC National Congress pointed out that China will step up efforts to establish a legal and policy framework that promotes green production and consumption, and promote a sound economic structure that facilitates green, low-carbon, and circular development. China will create a market-based system for green technology innovation, develop green finance, and encourage the development of energy-saving and environmental protection industries as well as clean production and clean energy industries. China will promote a revolution in energy production and consumption, and build an energy sector that is clean, low-carbon, safe and efficient.

China will encourage conservation across the board and promote recycling, take action to ensure that everyone conserves water, cut consumption of energy and materials, and establish linkages between the circular use of resources and materials in industrial production and in everyday life. China encourage simple, moderate, green, and low-carbon ways of life, and oppose extravagance and excessive consumption. China will launch initiatives to make Party and

色家庭、绿色学校、绿色社区和绿色出行等行动。

government offices do better when it comes to conservation, and develop eco-friendly families, schools, communities, and transport services.

生态文明体制改革

2012年11月，中共十八大提出，加快建立生态文明制度的战略部署。2013年11月，中共十八届三中全会提出，要加快建立系统完整的生态文明制度体系；2014年10月，十八届四中全会要求，用严格的法律制度保护生态环境；2015年9月，中共中央、国务院联合发布《生态文明体制改革总体方案》，从空间开发保护、资源总量管理、生态补偿、环境治理体系、绩效考核等8个方面作出顶层设计。中共十九大进一步提出，加快生态文明体制改革，建设美丽中国。同时部署了推进绿色发展、着力解决突出环境问题、加大生态系统保护力度、改革生态环境监管体制4项改革措施。中共十九大强调，加强对生态文明建设的总体设计和组织领导，设立国有自然资源资产管理和自然生态监管机构，完善生态环境管理制度，统一行使全民所有自然资源资产所有者职责，统一行使所有国土空间用途管制和生态保护修复职责，统一行使监管城乡各类污染排放和行政执法职责。构建国土空间开发保护制度，完善

Reform of the System for Developing an Ecological Civilization

In November 2012, the Party's 18th National Congress articulated its strategic vision for institution building for developing an ecological civilization. Related guidelines were unveiled in November 2013 by the 18th Central Committee at its third plenary session, and the need for an effective legal framework was highlighted in October 2014 at its fourth plenary session. An overall plan for institutional reform for developing an ecological civilization was jointly issued in September 2015 by the Party Central Committee and the State Council, outlining measures for protection against excessive development, total resource management, ecological compensation, environmental governance, and performance appraisal, among others.

The 19th CPC National Congress reaffirmed the importance of accelerating institutional reform for developing an ecological civilization and building a beautiful China, and specified reform measures, including promoting green development, tackling thorny environmental issues, strengthening the protection of ecosystems, and improving environmental oversight and monitoring.

It emphasized the need to strengthen overall planning and leadership for developing

主体功能区配套政策，建立以国家公园为主体的自然保护地体系。坚决制止和惩处破坏生态环境行为。

这些战略部署和重大举措，旨在提升生态环境领域国家治理体系和治理能力现代化水平；旨在从最棘手、最突出的生态环境问题入手，实施专项行动；旨在建立配套政策法规，改革组织架构。

an ecological civilization, and establish regulatory agencies to manage state-owned natural resource assets and monitor ecosystems. A unified environmental protection framework will be in place, under which oversight agencies are authorized to regulate the use of public-owned natural resource assets and land use, to impose appropriate measures to protect and restore ecosystems, and to monitor pollutant discharge amounts in urban and rural areas and take enforcement actions whenever and wherever necessary.

A complete system for land use regulation and protection against overdevelopment will include policies on functional zones and protected areas, especially national parks. Any activity that damages the ecosystems will be subject to punishment.

These strategic measures aim to enhance and modernize our national governance capacity for ecosystems protection, tackle the thorniest and most serious environmental challenges with targeted actions, and develop policies and laws that support ecosystems protection and improve related institutional structures.

打好污染防治的攻坚战

污染问题既是发展问题，又是民生问题，关系到全面建成小康社会的成效。污染防治，是制约中国全面建成小康社会的重点难点问题。2017年7月，习近平总书记在省部级主要领导干部专题研讨班上提出，突出抓重点、补短板、强弱项，特别是要坚决打好防范化解重大风险、精准扶贫、污染防治的攻坚战。党的十九大报告要求，坚持全民共治、源头防治，持续实施大气污染防治行动，打赢蓝天保卫战。加快水污染防治，实施流域环境和近岸海域综合治理。强化土壤污染管控和修复，加强农业面源污染防治，开展农村人居环境整治行动。加强固体废弃物和垃圾处置。提高污染排放标准，强化排污者责任，健全环保信用评价、信息强制性披露、严惩重罚等制度。构建政府为主导、

Protection Against Pollution

Pollution not only hinders development, but also erodes wellbeing and tends to thwart our efforts to realize the goal of building a moderately prosperous society. It has become a bottleneck issue that threatens to undercut our mission.

At a workshop for provincial officials in July 2017, General Secretary Xi Jinping affirmed the importance of addressing areas of weakness, especially conflict prevention and resolution, implementation of targeted anti-poverty measures, and protection against pollution.

The report to the 19th CPC National Congress called for a participatory approach to pollution reduction that tackles pollution at its source and encourages on-going efforts to prevent and control air pollution to make our skies blue again. Other measures are also indispensable, including prevention and control of water pollution, integrated river basin management and offshore resource management, soil pollution control and contaminated soil restoration, agricultural nonpoint pollution prevention and control, improvement of the rural living environment, and treatment of solid waste and garbage.

Stricter pollutant discharge standards will be enforced, and polluters will be held

企业为主体、社会组织和公众共同参与的环境治理体系。积极参与全球环境治理，落实减排承诺。

accountable. Other measures include credibility assessment for environmental protection, mandatory disclosure of environmental information, and punishment for violations of environmental laws and regulations. Also essential is building an environmental governance system, led by the government, with the business sector assuming main responsibility for reducing its environmental footprint, and with active participation of civil society actors and the public. We remain committed to global environmental governance, and our resolve to pursue emissions reduction is unshaken.

打赢蓝天保卫战

李克强总理在2017年政府工作报告中，明确提出了“坚决打好蓝天保卫战”的要求，提出了“2017年二氧化硫、氮氧化物排放量要分别下降3%，重点地区细颗粒物(PM2.5)浓度明显下降”的具体目标。为此，报告还提出了五方面举措：一要加快解决燃煤污染问题；二要全面推进污染源治理；三要强化机动车尾气治理；四要有效应对重污染天气；五要严格环境执法和督查问责。十九大报告进一步强调，坚持全民共治、源头防治，持续实施大气污染防治行动，打赢蓝天保卫战。蓝天保卫战要完成的是双重任务：到2020年，全国338个地级城市空气质量优良天数比率必须达到80%以上，这意味着以2015年为基数，未达标城市PM2.5浓度要平均下降18%；同时，还要为2035年生态环境根本改善的目标做好谋划、打好基础。从“打

Making China's Skies Blue Again

In his 2017 Report on the Work of the Government, Premier Li Keqiang vowed to "make our skies blue again." He specified that "this year, we will see that sulfur dioxide and nitrogen oxide emissions are both cut by 3 percent and that fine particulate matter (PM2.5) density in key areas falls markedly."

To this end, he demanded efforts to address pollution caused by coal burning, a full range of measures to improve the sources of pollution, strict control over exhaust fumes from motor vehicles, effective steps to combat heavy air pollution, strict enforcement of environmental laws and regulations, and investigations to identify violators and hold them accountable.

The report to the 19th National Congress of the CPC proposed involving everyone in improving the environment and addressing environmental issues at the root, and continuing the campaign to prevent and control air pollution and make the skies blue again.

There are two major tasks to fulfill: (1) By 2020, 338 prefecture-level cities across the country must see that their residents breathe fresh air on at least 80 percent of the days of the year, which means that there will be an 18 percent drop in the annual average density of

好”到“打赢”，既反映了党中央治理大气污染的坚定决心，也是对广大人民的庄严承诺。

fine particulate matter (PM2.5) in those cities that failed to meet relevant standard in 2015; (2) There must be good planning and sound foundations to secure a fundamental improvement of the environment by 2035.

The pledge to make the skies blue again reflects the firm determination of the CPC Central Committee to control air pollution and meet the people's expectation.

生态保护红线

生态红线，亦称生态保护红线，是指在自然生态服务功能、环境质量安全、自然资源利用等方面，需要实行严格保护的空间边界与管理限值，以维护国家和区域生态安全及经济社会可持续发展、保障人民群众健康。生态红线是国家生态安全的底线和生命线，这个红线不能突破，一旦突破后果必将危及生态安全、人民生产生活和国家可持续发展。中国政府正在通过精心研究和论证，确定究竟哪些要列入生态红线，如何从制度上保障生态红线，把良好生态环境尽可能保护起来。生态红线一旦确立，全国就要一体遵行，决不能逾越。

Ecological Red Lines

Ecological red lines, also known as "conservation red lines," refer to spatial boundaries and environmental management limits that must be strictly observed in ecological conservation services, environmental quality and safety controls, and natural resource utilization, in order to ensure national and regional ecological safety, sustainable economic and social development, and people's health.

These lines are essential for securing China's ecological safety, and must not be crossed. Otherwise the country's ecology, the people's working and living conditions, and sustainable development will all be endangered.

The Chinese government is conducting research on the delineation of red lines and their effective implementation through institutional arrangements, so as to offer the best possible protection for a healthy environment. Once the mechanism of red lines is in place, it must be implemented throughout the country without fail.

生态补偿制度

中共十八届三中全会《决定》提出实行生态补偿制度。生态补偿制度，是以防止生态环境破坏、增强和促进生态系统良性发展为目的，以从事对生态环境产生或可能产生影响的生产、经营、开发、利用者为对象，以生态环境整治及恢复为主要内容，以经济调节为手段，以法律为保障的新型环境管理制度。它可分为广义和狭义两种。广义包括对污染环境的补偿和对生态功能的补偿，狭义则专指对生态功能或生态价值的补偿。中国政府将坚持谁污染环境、谁破坏生态谁付费和谁受益谁补偿原则，完善对重点生态功能区的生态补

Eco-Compensation System

The decision to establish an eco-compensation system was made by the 18th CPC Central Committee at its third plenary session. The system aims to prevent damage to the environment, and enhance and promote ecological conservation and protection. It targets those involved in business and other activities, including production, exploitation, and use of natural resources, which has or might have negative environmental impacts. It represents a new approach to environmental stewardship that relies on market-based mechanisms and a legal framework to promote the management of ecosystem protection and restoration.

The eco-compensation approach can be understood in both a broad and a narrow sense. Broadly speaking, it involves compensation for environmental pollution or for damage to ecosystem functions. In a narrow sense, it refers specifically to compensation for damage to ecosystem functions and their value.

The Chinese government will implement the "polluter pays" principle to make those who produce pollution and benefit therefrom responsible for paying for the damage done to the environment. Efforts will be stepped up to improve the compensation mechanism for key

偿机制，推动地区间建立横向生态补偿制度。

ecosystem function conservation areas and to establish cross- regional eco-compensation programs.

坚持走中国特色强军之路，全面推进国防和军队现代化

Staying Committed to the Chinese Path of Building Strong Armed Forces and Fully Advancing the Modernization of National Defense and the Military

中国特色强军之路

2015年11月24日，习近平在中央军委改革工作会议上提出全面实施改革强军战略，坚定不移走中国特色强军之路的要求。深化国防和军队改革，是实现中国梦强军梦的时代要求，是强军兴军的必由之路，也是决定军队未来的关键一招。改革的目标就是构建能够打赢信息化战争、有效履行使命任务的中国特色现代军事力量体系，使中国特色社会主义军事制度更加成熟、更加定型，为实现强军目标、建设世界一流军队打下更为扎实的前进基础。改革的成果标志，就是在领导管理体制、联合作战指挥体制改革上取得突破性进展，在优化规模结构和力量编成、完善政策制度、推动军民融合发展等方面改革上取得重要成果。改革的六方面举措包括：一是形成军委管总、战区主战、军种主建的格局；二是构建严密的权力运行制约和监督体系；三是推动人民解放军由数量规

Chinese Path of Building Strong Armed Forces

At a meeting of the Central Military Commission (CMC) on military reform on November 24, 2015, Xi Jinping emphasized the importance of implementing a strategy to build a strong military through reform, by taking a distinctly Chinese approach. Reforming national defense and the armed forces is essential to realizing the Chinese Dream and the dream of building a powerful military, to strengthening and revitalizing the armed forces, and to shaping the future of China's military.

The objectives include overhauling leadership and joint operational command structures, optimizing the size and composition of the armed forces, establishing a sound framework for policy-making, and improving civil-military integration. The result will be a modern military that meets China's need to safeguard its socialist development by being ready and able to answer the call of duty and win a war in a digital age. This will lay a solid foundation for the goal of building a strong world-class military.

Major measures include:

• building a structure with the CMC providing overall guidance and direction, theater commands responsible for theater-level combat operations, and individual

模型向质量效能型转变；四是培育军队战斗力新的增长点；五是推动人才发展体制改革和政策创新；六是推动经济建设和国防建设融合发展。

military services focused on their specialized combat capability and readiness;

• designing an effective oversight system to prevent any abuse of power;

• shifting from reliance on the size of the military to a focus on quality and efficiency;

• identifying and tapping new potential for warfare capability improvement and force multiplication;

• pursuing institutional reform and policy innovation in talent and human resource development; and

• integrating economic development with defense needs.

新时代党的强军思想

建设一支强大的人民军队，必须要有先进思想引领、科学理论指导。党的十八大以来，习近平作为党的领袖、军队统帅，着眼实现中国梦强军梦，作出一系列重大决策部署，创立了新时代党的强军思想，引领军队开启强军兴军新征程，推动军队面貌发生前所未有的历史性变化，可谓“凤凰涅槃”“浴火重生”“重塑再造”。党的十九大报告明确提出，要确立新时代党的强军思想在国防和军队建设中的指导地位。这一思想主要包含以下内容：一是“建设一支听党指挥、能打胜仗、作风优良的人民军队”的强军目标；二是“五个更加注重”的战略指导，即：更加注重聚焦实战，更加注重创新驱动，更加注重体系建设，更加注重集约高效，更加注重军民融合；三是永葆人民军队的本色初心；四是向深化国防和军队改革要动力；五是坚持向科技创新要战斗力；六是全面提升国防和军队建设的法治化水平；七是始终聚焦军队的主责主业；八是夯实强军兴军的

The Party's Vision for Building a Strong Military for a New Era

Efforts to build strong people's armed forces need to be guided by a forward-looking vision, and proceed on a solid theoretical basis. Since the Party's 18th National Congress, Xi Jinping as the leader of the Party and commander-in-chief of the armed forces has proposed a series of major policy decisions as part of an overall strategy for building a strong military for a new era. He has in particular laid out our Party's vision that guides us on a new journey to remake our military, an unprecedented effort of historic significance that will propel our military to further greatness.

The report to the 19th CPC National Congress underlines the importance of this vision to the efforts to strengthen our defense capability. The vision calls for:

- affirming the leadership role of the Party in building a strong, well-disciplined military able to fight and win major wars;
- keeping a strategic focus on combat capability and readiness, innovative measures, institutional strengthening, development of a more efficient, integrated command structure, and military-civilian integration;
- staying true to the founding mission of

人才支撑。

新时代党的强军思想，是习近平新时代中国特色社会主义思想的重要组成部分，深刻回答了新时代“人民军队听谁指挥、怎样铸牢军魂”“为什么强军、怎样强军”、“打什么仗、怎样打胜仗”等基本问题，丰富发展了我们党建军治军思想和方针原则，指引了人民军队的强军新征程。

the people's armed forces;

• implementing further reform;

• promoting scientific and technological innovation to upgrade our fighting power;

• enhancing rule-based governance of the military;

• staying focused on what the military is supposed to do without being distracted; and

• implementing an effective talent strategy.

This vision is an important component of Xi Jinping Thought on Socialism with Chinese Characteristics for a New Era. It answers the basic questions about under whose command our people's armed forces should be, how the Party's leadership role – which is the soul of the military – can be strengthened, why we have to build a strong military and how we can achieve this goal, and what we should be prepared for and how we can strengthen combat capability. It enriches our Party's guiding principles for governance of the military, and guides us toward new horizons.

新形势下军事战略方针

2015年5月，中国政府发布了《中国的军事战略》白皮书，提出了实行新形势下积极防御军事战略方针坚持的原则。这些原则是：服从服务于国家战略目标，贯彻总体国家安全观，加强军事斗争准备，预防危机、遏制战争、打赢战争；营造有利于国家和平发展的战略态势，坚持防御性国防政策，坚持政治、军事、经济、外交等领域斗争密切配合，积极应对国家可能面临的综合安全威胁；保持维权维稳平衡，统筹维权和维稳两个大局，维护国家领土主权和海洋权益，维护周边安全稳定；努力争取军事斗争战略主动，积极运筹谋划各方向各领域军事斗争，抓住机遇加快推进军队建设、改革和发展；运用灵活机动的战略战术，发挥联合作战整体效能，集中优势力量，综合运用战法手段；立足应对最复杂最困难情况，坚持底线思维，扎实做好各项准备工作，确保妥善应对、措置裕如；充分发挥人民军队特有的政治优势，坚持党对军队的绝对领导，重视战

China's Military Strategic Guideline for a New Era

In May 2015, the Chinese government published a white paper titled *China's Military Strategy*, which defined the strategic guideline of active defense for a new era.

To implement the guideline, China's armed forces will uphold the following principles:

• To be subordinate to and in the service of national strategic goals, implement a holistic view of national security, strengthen PMS, prevent crises, and deter or win wars;

• To foster a strategic posture favorable to China's peaceful development, adhere to the national defense policy that is defensive in nature, persevere in close coordination of political, military, economic and diplomatic work, and positively deal with comprehensive security threats the country possibly encounters;

• To strike a balance between protecting rights and maintaining stability, and make an overall plan for both, to safeguard national territorial sovereignty and maritime rights and interests, and to maintain security and stability along China's periphery;

• To endeavor to seize the strategic initiative in any military conflict, to build proactive plans to deal with any potential for military conflict, and to accelerate military reform and

斗精神培育，严格部队组织纪律性，纯洁巩固部队，密切军政军民关系，鼓舞军心士气；发挥人民战争的整体威力，坚持把人民战争作为克敌制胜的重要法宝，拓展人民战争的内容和方式方法，推动战争动员以人力动员为主向以科技动员为主转变；积极拓展军事安全合作空间，深化与大国、周边、发展中国家的军事关系，促进建立地区安全和合作架构。

development;

• To employ flexible and mobile strategies and tactics, give full play to the overall effectiveness of joint operations, concentrate superior forces, and integrate all operational means and methods;

• To make serious preparations to deal with the most complex and difficult scenarios, uphold bottom-line thinking, and ensure the ability to respond with ease to such scenarios, at any time and in any circumstances;

• To bring into full play the unique political strengths of the people's armed forces, uphold the CPC's absolute leadership over the military, accentuate the cultivation of fighting spirit, enforce strict discipline, improve the professionalism and strength of the troops, build closer relations between the government and the military as well as between the people and the military, and boost the morale of officers and men;

• To give full play to the overall power of people's war, persevere in employing it as an ace weapon to triumph over the enemy, enrich the contents, ways and means of the concept of people's war;

• To shift the focus of war mobilization from human resources to science and technology; and

• To actively expand military and security cooperation, to extend military relations with major powers, neighboring countries, and other developing countries, and to promote a regional framework for security and cooperation.

国防和军队现代化

党的十九大报告提出，中国的国防和军队建设正站在新的历史起点上。面对国家安全环境的深刻变化，面对强国强军的时代要求，必须全面贯彻新时代党的强军思想，贯彻新形势下军事战略方针，建设强大的现代化陆军、海军、空军、火箭军和战略支援部队，打造坚强高效的战区联合作战指挥机构，构建中国特色现代作战体系，担当起党和人民赋予的新时代使命任务。国防和军队建设的三个阶段性目标是：确保到2020年基本实现机械化，信息化建设取得重大进展，战略能力有大的提升。同国家现代化进程相一致，全面推进军事理论现代化、军队组织形态现代化、军事人员现代化、武器装备现代化，力争

Modernization of National Defense and the Military

As stated in the report to the 19th CPC National Congress, we have now reached a new starting point in our efforts to strengthen national defense and the armed forces. Profound changes in the national security landscape lead to new imperatives for building a strong country with a strong military. Guided by the Party's vision for strengthening the military for a new era, we must adapt our military strategy to new conditions, and build powerful, modern armed forces, including the army, the navy, the air force, the missile forces, and the strategic support forces. It is essential to develop an efficient joint operational command chain for theater commands, as part of the effort to build our modern warfare capabilities with Chinese characteristics to meet new challenges in the new era and to accomplish the mission entrusted by the Party and the people.

Modernization of national defense and the military will be accomplished in three stages. By the year 2020, mechanization will be basically achieved, with significantly expanded use of information technology and significantly upgraded strategic capabilities. The process will proceed in lockstep with our country's modernization drive, and cover all

到2035年基本实现国防和军队现代化，到本世纪中叶把人民军队全面建成世界一流军队。

aspects of our defense needs including military theory, organizational structures, service personnel training and combat readiness, and weaponry. By 2035, defense modernization will be basically completed. By the mid-21st century, the armed forces will be transformed into a world-class fighting force.

坚持“一国两制”，推进祖国统一

Upholding “One Country, Two Systems” and Moving Toward National Reunification

“九二共识”

“九二共识”的缘起是为实现和推进两岸协商奠定政治基础。1992年10月底至12月初，中国大陆的民间团体——海峡两岸关系协会与中国台湾的民间团体——海峡交流基金会，经过多次磋商，最终形成了以口头方式表达的“海峡两岸均坚持一个中国的原则”的共识，后被称为“九二共识”。其核心是“坚持一个中国”，精髓是求同存异。“九二共识”明确界定了两岸关系的根本性质，即大陆与台湾同属一个中国，两岸关系不是国与国关系，也不是“一中一台”。“九二共识”是两岸关系保持和平稳定和良性互动的基础，是确保两岸关系和平发展的关键。承认“九二共识”的历史事实，认同两岸同属一个中国，两岸双方就能开展对话，协商解决两岸同胞关心的问题，台湾任何政党和团体同大陆交往也不会存在障碍。正是以“九二共识”为基础，才实现了2005年4月在北京举行

The "1992 Consensus"

The "1992 Consensus" was an oral agreement reached between the mainland-based Association for Relations Across the Taiwan Straits (ARATS) and the Taiwan-based Straits Exchange Foundation (SEF), resulting from talks they held between late October and early December of 1992. The two non-governmental organizations agreed that "both sides of the Taiwan Straits will follow the one-China principle," and this subsequently became the political foundation for cross-Straits consultations.

The kernel of the 1992 Consensus is the "one-China principle," which means seeking common ground while reserving differences. The "1992 Consensus" defines cross-Straits relations as neither "state-to-state" nor "one China, one Taiwan," but confirms the fact that the mainland and Taiwan belong to one China.

The "1992 Consensus" is the foundation on which cross-Straits relations can progress positively in peace and stability. It therefore holds the key to peaceful development between the two sides of the Taiwan Straits. By recognizing the "1992 Consensus" and accepting that the two sides both belong to one China, both sides can conduct dialog to address through discussion the concerns of the people of both sides, and no political party or group in Taiwan will have any difficulty in

的国共两党领导人历史性会谈，以及2015年11月在新加坡举行的两岸领导人历史性会晤。

conducting exchanges with the mainland.

It was on this basis that the historic discussions between the leaders of the CPC and the KMT were conducted in Beijing in April 2005, and the historic meeting between the leaders from both sides of the Taiwan Straits was held in Singapore in November 2015.

“两岸一家亲”

两岸同胞是命运与共的骨肉兄弟，是血浓于水的一家人。习近平对台湾问题有深刻的理解，熟知台湾历史和两岸关系历程，也理解台湾同胞因其历史遭遇和社会环境所形成的特定心态，多次表达了愿与台湾同胞一起努力，化解台湾同胞的历史心结、共同把握现在、开创未来的真诚心愿。2013年4月8日，他在海南博鳌会见台湾两岸共同市场基金会荣誉董事长萧万长时提出，希望本着“两岸一家人”的理念促进两岸经济合作。此后，他又多次强调和践行“两岸一家亲”理念。两岸同胞一家亲，根植于同胞共同的血脉和精神，扎根于两岸共同的历史和文化。习近平从血脉亲情、历史文化、民族复兴的角度提出“两岸一家亲”，指明了两岸同胞处理彼此关系的基本思路，有助于拉近两岸同胞的感情和心理距离，增进共同的国家、民族、文化认同，共圆中华民族复兴的中

People on Both Sides of the Taiwan Strait Are All of the Same Family

Xi Jinping has a deep understanding of the Taiwan question and is familiar with the history of Taiwan and cross-strait relations. He understands the specific concerns of the people in Taiwan, with what happened in the past and the specific position they now find themselves in. He has, therefore, expressed his sincere desire on many occasions to work with the people in Taiwan to help allay the historical misgivings that may still exist in Taiwan so that people on both sides could join hands and move to the future.

On April 8, 2013, in Bo'ao, Hainan Province, he met with Mr. Vincent Siew, honorary chairman of the Cross-Strait Common Market Foundation, and expressed his hope that two sides could work together as "one family" and increase their economic cooperation. On numerous occasions afterward, he again emphasized the idea of "ties of kinship between the two sides." This bond is rooted in our blood and soul, and in the history and culture we share. Xi Jinping proposed the idea of "ties of kinship" based on this close bond, on our common history and culture, and on our goal of national rejuvenation.

As the guideline for advancing relations between people on both sides of the Taiwan

国梦。2015年11月7日，两岸领导人习近平、马英九在新加坡香格里拉大酒店的历史性会面，正是“两岸一家亲”的最真实写照。

Strait, this idea of kinship helps shorten their emotional and psychological distance so that people on both sides can work together with stronger recognition of our shared national, ethnic, and cultural identity, in our drive to achieve the Chinese Dream of national rejuvenation. The historical meeting between Xi Jinping and Ma Ying-jeou, leaders from both sides of the Taiwan Strait, at the Shangri-La Hotel in Singapore, was a good example of this family bond between the two sides.

坚持和平发展道路，推动构建人类命运共同体

Following a Path of Peaceful Development and Working to Build a Community with a Shared Future for Humanity

中国特色大国外交

中国共产党是为中国人民谋幸福的政党，也是为人类进步事业而奋斗的政党。中国共产党始终把为人类作出新的更大的贡献作为自己的使命。2014年11月，习近平在中央外事工作会议上指出，中国必须有自己的特色大国外交。党的十九大报告强调，中国特色大国外交要推动构建新型国际关系，推动构建人类命运共同体。为此，中国将高举和平、发展、合作、共赢的旗帜，推动建设互相尊重、公平正义、合作共赢的新型国际关系；呼吁各国人民同心协力，构建人类命运共同体，建设持久和平、普遍安全、共同繁荣、开放包容、清洁美丽的世界；坚定奉行独立自主的和平外交政策，反对干涉别国内政，反对以强凌弱；中国绝不会以牺牲别国利益为代价来发展自己，也绝不放弃自己的正当权益，任何人不要幻想让中国吞下损害自身利益的苦果；奉行防御性的国防政策，中国发展不对任何国家构成威胁；积极发展全球伙伴关系，扩大同各国的利益交汇点；坚持对外开放的基本国策，坚持

Major Country Diplomacy with Chinese Characteristics

The CPC is committed to improving the wellbeing of the Chinese people, and to advancing human progress. It has always been our mission to contribute to humanity's progress. To this end, a proactive foreign policy that reflects China's position as a major country with Chinese characteristics is critical, as Xi Jinping stated at the Central Committee's Foreign Policy Meeting in November 2014.

The report to the 19th CPC National Congress underlined the importance of such a policy and its role in building a new form of international relations and a community with a shared future for humanity.

China's commitment to peace, development, cooperation, and mutual benefit remains unshaken, and the new form of international relations we envisage is based on mutual respect, fairness, justice, and cooperation for mutual benefit.

China calls on all countries and people all over the world to work together to build a community with a shared future for humanity, an open, inclusive, clean, and beautiful world that enjoys lasting peace, universal security, and shared prosperity.

China will never falter in its pursuit

打开国门搞建设；秉持共商共建共享的全球治理观，倡导国际关系民主化；将继续发挥负责任大国作用，积极参与全球治理体系改革和建设，不断贡献中国智慧和力量。

of an independent foreign policy of peace. It opposes any interference in the internal affairs of other countries or power politics that subjects the weak to bullying.

China will never pursue development at the expense of other countries' interests; nor will China ever give up its legitimate rights and interests. No one should expect China to swallow anything that undermines its interests. China pursues a national defense policy that is in nature defensive. China's development does not pose a threat to any other country.

China will continue to forge global partnerships that reflect and promote convergence of interests, and remain committed to an open-door policy in our development efforts. Guided by our vision for participatory global governance, we encourage greater democracy in international relations, and will actively participate in and contribute to global governance reform as a responsible member of the international community.

新型国际关系

2013年3月，习近平在莫斯科国际关系学院演讲时提出，“各国应该共同推动建立以合作共赢为核心的新型国际关系”。当今世界正在发生深刻复杂的变化，和平、发展、合作、共赢的时代潮流更加强劲，但维护世界和平、促进共同发展，依然任重道远。今天的人类比以往任何时候都更有条件朝和平与发展的目标迈进，而合作共赢就是实现这一目标的现实途径。中国倡导建立合作共赢的新型国际关系，核心是维护联合国宪章的宗旨和原则，维护不干涉内政和尊重国家主权、独立、领土完整等国际关系基本准则，维护联合国及其安理会对世界和平承担的首要责任，开展对话和合作，而不是对抗；实现双赢和共赢，而不是单赢。构建以合作共赢为核心的新型国际关系，需要建立平等相待、互商互谅的伙伴关系，营造公道正义、共建共享的安全格局，谋求开放创新、包容互惠的发展前景，促进和而不同、兼收并蓄的文明交流，构筑尊崇自然、绿色发展的生态体系。构建新型国际关系，必须坚持和平发展，摒弃强权和战争；必须遵循多

A New Form of International Relations

In an address at the Moscow State Institute of International Relations in March 2013, Xi Jinping brought up this idea for the first time. He said, "All countries should join hands in building a new form of international relations characterized by cooperation and mutual benefit."

The world today is in a period of profound and complex changes, and the trend of the times – peace, development, cooperation and mutual benefit – is gaining momentum. But upholding world peace and promoting common development remain a long and uphill battle. Mankind has never been better blessed to take strides toward peace and development, and mutually beneficial cooperation provides the only practical way to achieve such a goal.

China advocates a new form of international relations based on cooperation for the benefit of all. In building such a model, countries should follow the purposes and principles of the Charter of the United Nations, observe the basic rules governing international relations, such as not interfering in the internal affairs of other countries and respecting each other's sovereignty, independence and territorial integrity, support the primary role of the UN and its Security Council in defending

边主义，推进国际关系民主化和法治化；必须改革完善全球经济治理，建设开放型世界经济；必须建立新型全球发展伙伴关系，让发展成果公平惠及地球每个角落。

world peace, and engage in dialog and cooperation instead confrontation, so as to achieve win-win and all-win rather than one-win results.

To build a new form of international relations based on cooperation for the benefit of all, the international community needs to build partnerships based on equality, consultation and mutual understanding, to create a security architecture that is fair, just and shared by all, to pursue open, innovative and inclusive development that benefits all, to increase inter-civilizational exchanges that promote harmony in diversity and are mutually enriching, and to encourage ecological conservation and protection, putting Mother Nature and green development first.

To this end, the world must pursue peaceful development rather than power politics and war, promote multilateralism and democracy in international relations based on rule of law, reform and improve global economic governance, build an open world economy, and foster a new form of global partnership for development. Then development will be of benefit to every corner of the Earth.

“一带一路”倡议

“一带一路”是“丝绸之路经济带”和“21世纪海上丝绸之路”的简称。2013年9月和10月，习近平出访中亚和东南亚时，分别提出了与相关国家共同建设“丝绸之路经济带”和“21世纪海上丝绸之路”的倡议。建设“一带一路”，是党中央作出的重大决策，是实施新一轮扩大开放的重要举措。该倡议以实现“政策沟通、设施联通、贸易畅通、资金融通、民心相通”为主要内容，以“共商、共建、共享”为原则，以“利益共同体、责任共同体、命运共同体”为目标。要将“一带一路”建成和平之路、繁荣之路、开放之路、创新之路、文明之路。“一带一路”建设符合有关各方共同利益，顺应地区和全球合作潮流，得到了沿线国家的积极响应。4年来，全球100多个国家和国际组织积极支持和参与“一带一路”建设，联合国大会、联合国安理会等重要决议也纳入“一带一路”建设内容。“一带一路”建设逐渐从理念转化为行动，从愿景转变为现实，建设成果丰硕。

The Belt and Road Initiative

The Belt and Road Initiative – China's proposal to cooperate with other countries in building a Silk Road Economic Belt and a 21st Century Maritime Silk Road – was unveiled by President Xi Jinping during his visits to Central and Southeast Asia in September and October 2013. It was a strategic decision taken by the central leadership as part of a new process of further opening up to the outside world.

The initiative focuses on policy coordination, connectivity of infrastructure and facilities, unimpeded trade, financial integration, and strengthened people-to-people ties through a consultative process and joint efforts, with the goal of bringing benefits to all. It aims to build a community of shared interests and responsibility with a shared future. The Belt and Road will be a path to peace, prosperity and openness through innovative programs and friendly engagement.

Over the past four years, more than 100 countries and international organizations have expressed support for the initiative and participated in related activities. The UN General Assembly and Security Council have also made reference to the initiative in some of their resolutions. The vision of the Belt and Road is gradually being translated into action, and success stories have begun to emerge.

亚洲基础设施投资银行

2013 年 10 月，习近平提出了筹建亚洲基础设施投资银行（简称亚投行）的倡议。在历经800 余天筹备后，由中国倡议成立、57 国共同筹建的亚投行于 2015 年 12 月 25 日在北京宣告成立。2016 年 1 月 16 日，亚投行举行了开业仪式。亚投行是一个政府间性质的区域多边开发机构，重点支持基础设施建设，这是首个由中国倡议设立的多边金融机构。截止到 2017 年 6月底，共有 80 个成员，总成员数仅次于世界银行，涵盖了联合国安理会常任理事国和二十国集团中的绝大多数成员国。亚投行作为多边开发银行有其单独的业务标准，“一带一路” 沿线国家都可以获得亚投行的贷款，但必须满足三个条件：一是金融可持续发展，二是项目要环保，三是项目要受到该地区民众的欢迎。亚投行初期投资重点领域包括能源与电力、交通和电信、农村和农业基础设施、供水与污水处理、环境保护、城市发展以及物流等。

Asian Infrastructure Investment Bank

The idea of creating a new multilateral bank, the Asian Infrastructure Investment Bank (AIIB), was first evoked by Xi Jinping in October 2013. After more than 800 days of combined preparatory efforts by 57 countries, the AIIB was formally established, in accordance with China's proposal, on December 25, 2015 in Beijing. The bank held its opening ceremony on January 16, 2016.

The AIIB is a regional inter-governmental development institution focused on supporting infrastructure development. It is the first multinational financial institution to be sponsored by China. By the end of June 2017 it had a total of 80 members – second only to the membership of the World Bank – including most UN Security Council permanent members and G20 members.

As a multilateral development bank, the AIIB operates according to its own standards. All countries along the Belt and Road can obtain loans, provided that their projects (a) are financially viable, (b) are environmentally friendly, and (c) have the support of local communities.

Among other sectors, the bank is initially investing in energy and electricity, transport, telecommunications, rural and agricultural infrastructure, water supply and sewerage,

截止到2017年11月，亚投行共批准了21个项目，总金额为34.9亿美元。

environmental protection, urban development, and logistics. As of November 2017, 21 projects have been approved to a total value of US$3.49 billion.

丝路基金

2014年11月8日，习近平宣布，中国将出资400亿美元成立丝路基金。2014年12月29日，丝路基金有限责任公司在北京注册成立。丝路基金秉承“开放包容、互利共赢”的理念，是中长期开发投资基金，重点为“一带一路”沿线国基础设施建设、资源开发、产业合作等有关项目提供投融资支持。它同其他全球和区域多边开发银行的关系是相互补充而不是相互替代的。它将在现行国际经济金融秩序下运行。丝路基金绝非简单的经济援助，而是通过互联互通为相关国家的发展创造新的重大发展机遇。丝路基金是开放的，欢迎亚洲域内外的投资者积极参与。

Silk Road Fund

Following Xi Jinping's announcement on November 8, 2014 that China would contribute US$40 billion for this purpose, the Silk Road Fund was established in Beijing on December 29, 2014. Guided by the principles of openness, inclusiveness, and mutual benefit, the Fund focuses on providing medium- to long-term loans to support infrastructure and resource development and industrial cooperation in the countries along the Belt and Road. It complements rather than replaces other global and regional multilateral development banks, and operates under the existing international economic and financial order.

Rather than simply dispensing economic aid, the Fund will take advantage of increased connectivity to create major development opportunities for all. It is an open program and welcomes the participation of investors from Asia and beyond.

全球伙伴关系

党的十九大报告强调，中国积极发展全球伙伴关系，扩大同各国的利益交汇点，推进大国协调和合作，构建总体稳定、均衡发展的大国关系框架，按照亲诚惠容理念和与邻为善、以邻为伴周边外交方针深化同周边国家关系，秉持正确义利观和真实亲诚理念加强同发展中国家团结合作。加强同各国政党和政治组织的交流合作，推进人大、政协、军队、地方、人民团体等的对外交往。近年来，中国积极构建对话而不对抗、结伴而不结盟的全球伙伴关系网络。截至2016年底,中国已经同97个国家和国际组织建立了不同形式的伙

Global Partnerships

As stated in the report to the 19th CPC National Congress, China has actively developed global partnerships and expanded the convergence of interests with other countries. China will promote coordination and cooperation with other major countries and work to build a framework for major country relations featuring overall stability and balanced development. China will deepen relations with its neighbors in accordance with the principle of amity, sincerity, mutual benefit, and inclusiveness and the policy of forging friendship and partnership with its neighbors. China will, guided by the principle of upholding justice while pursuing shared interests and the principle of sincerity, real results, affinity, and good faith, work to strengthen solidarity and cooperation with other developing countries.

We will strengthen exchanges and cooperation with the political parties and organizations of other countries, and encourage people's congresses, CPPCC committees, the military, local governments, and people's organizations to engage in exchanges with other countries.

In recent years, China has been making great efforts to build a global network of cooperation that encourages dialog instead of confrontation, and helps forge partnerships instead of antagonistic blocs.

As of the end of 2016, China had

伴关系，全球“朋友圈”不断扩展，实现全球覆盖。

established various forms of partnership relations with 97 countries and international organizations. Our circle of friends has been expanding globally.

亲、诚、惠、容的理念

2013年10月24日，习近平在周边外交工作座谈会上强调，中国周边外交的基本方针，就是坚持与邻为善、以邻为伴，坚持睦邻、安邻、富邻，突出体现亲、诚、惠、容的理念。亲是指巩固地缘相近、人缘相亲的友好情谊，要坚持睦邻友好、守望相助，讲平等、重感情，常见面、多走动，多做得人心、暖人心的事，使周边国家对我们更友善、更亲近、更认同、更支持，增强亲和力、感召力、影响力。诚是指坚持以诚待人、以信取人的相处之道，要诚心诚意对待周边国家，争取更多朋友和伙伴。惠是指履行惠及周边、互利共赢的合作理念，要本着互惠互利的原则同周边国家开展合作，编织更加紧密的共同利益网络，把双方利益融合提升到更高水平，让周边国家得益于我国发展，使我国也从周边国家共同发展中获得裨益和助力。容是指展示开放包容、求同存异

Building Relations with Neighboring Countries Based on Amity, Sincerity, Mutual Benefit and Inclusiveness

At a seminar on relations with neighboring countries on October 24, 2013, Xi Jinping described China's neighborhood diplomacy as one rooted in the principles for building strong relations with its neighbors based on amity, sincerity, mutual benefit and inclusiveness.

Friendship involves good-neighborly interactions, mutual support and assistance, and frequent reciprocal visits, and is informed by equality, cultural affinity, and empathy. The more we do to win the hearts and minds of our neighbors, the stronger our ties will become. Strengthened amity helps us win support for the goals we pursue on the world stage, and enhances our appeal and our influence in world affairs. Sincerity is indispensable if we want to work with and win trust from our neighbors. We need more friends and partners. Mutual benefit is the foundation on which China cooperates with its neighbors. It helps strengthen networks for those who share common interests, and enables China and its neighbors to benefit from each other as they pursue their development strategies.

的大国胸怀，要倡导包容的思想，强调亚太之大容得下大家共同发展，以更加开放的胸襟和更加积极的态度促进地区合作。亲、诚、惠、容这“四字箴言”，是新形势下中国坚持走和平发展道路的一份生动宣言，是对多年来中国周边外交实践的一个精辟概括，也反映了中国新一届中央领导集体外交理念的创新发展。

Inclusiveness is key to regional cooperation. Underpinned by the belief that the Asia-Pacific region is large enough to accommodate us all, it encourages open-mindedness as we work more proactively toward our shared goals.

The emphasis on amity, sincerity, mutual benefit and inclusiveness represents the essence of China's policy of good-neighborliness, as part of China's peaceful development strategy. It also reflects the fresh thinking on foreign policy of China's new leadership.

正确义利观

党的十八大以来，习近平多次强调在外交工作中要坚持正确义利观。义，反映的是我们的一个理念。中国希望全世界共同发展，特别是希望广大发展中国家加快发展。利，就是要恪守互利共赢原则，不搞我赢你输，要实现双赢。中国有义务对贫穷的国家给予力所能及的帮助，有时甚至要重义轻利、舍利取义，绝不能唯利是图、斤斤计较。树立和贯彻正确义利观，就是有原则、讲情义、讲道义，见利思义、义利兼得，甚至必要时舍利取义；正确义利观体现了中华民族传统美德和中国外交优良品格，进一步丰富了中国外交的价值观，得到国际社会特别是广大发展中

Upholding Justice While Pursuing Shared Interests

Since the 18th CPC National Congress, Xi Jinping has on many occasions emphasized the importance of upholding justice and pursuing shared interests in our foreign relations. This reflects our values. China hopes to see common prosperity across the world and, in particular, accelerated development in developing countries.

The pursuit of shared interests should be aligned with the need to search for mutual benefit, rather than being turned into a zero-sum game. China has the obligation to provide assistance to poor countries within the limits of its own resources. It is sometimes necessary to work for justice at the expense of self-interest and fulfill this obligation despite an unfavorable calculus in financial terms.

A healthy approach to the relationship between upholding justice and pursuing shared interests is a principled approach that values friendship, adheres to moral standards, refuses to succumb to the temptations of greed, encourages us to seek gain only when justice is not adversely affected, and embraces a readiness to sacrifice self-interest for justice when need arises. This approach is grounded in traditional Chinese culture and our foreign policy thinking, and embodies the

国家的普遍赞誉，成为中国软实力的独特标志。

values we cherish. It has won praise from the international community in general and from developing countries in particular. It is a manifestation of China's soft power.

真、实、亲、诚的理念

2013年3月，习近平在达累斯萨拉姆发表演讲时，全面阐述中非关系以及中国对非政策主张：第一，对待非洲朋友，讲一个“真”字，始终把发展同非洲国家的团结合作作为中国对外政策的重要基础。第二，开展对非合作，讲一个“实”字，只要是中方作出的承诺，就一定会不折不扣落到实处。第三，加强中非友好，讲一个“亲”字。中非人民有着天然的亲近感，要更加重视中非人文交流，积极推动青年交流，使中非友好事业后继有人。第四，解决合作中的问题，讲一个“诚”字，中方坦诚面对中非关系面临的新情况新问题，本着相互尊重、合作共赢的精神加以妥善解决。不仅对非洲，真实亲诚理念已经成为中国与所有发展中国家加强团结合作时坚持的重要理念。

The Principle of Sincerity, Real Results, Affinity, and Good Faith

In his speech in Dar es Salaam, Tanzania, in March 2013, Xi Jinping elaborated on Sino-African relations and China's African policy.

China has a sincere desire to build strong ties with its African friends. Solidarity and cooperation with African countries has always been an important element of China's foreign policy.

Cooperation with Africa has been and will continue to be results-oriented. China will honor every commitment it makes to Africa.

The traditional and intimate friendship between the Chinese and African peoples will continue to strengthen. Efforts will be made to expand people-to-people exchanges, especially youth exchange programs, so that our friendship can be passed on to younger generations.

We will always act in good faith in addressing problems that might occur in our relations with Africa. New developments and issues relating to our bilateral relations will be discussed frankly and dealt with on the basis of mutual respect and through mutually beneficial cooperation.This principle has become an important practice in the cooperation between China and other developing countries.

全球治理观

2014年6月28日，习近平在和平共处五项原则发表60周年纪念大会上的讲话中提出，要适应国际力量对比新变化，推进全球治理体系改革的倡议。随着全球性挑战增多，加强全球治理、推进全球治理体制变革已是大势所趋。这不仅事关应对各种全球性挑战，而且事关给国际秩序和国际体系定规则、定方向；不仅事关对发展制高点的争夺，而且事关各国在国际秩序和国际体系长远制度性安排中的地位和作用。全球治理格局取决于国际力量对比，全球治理体系变革源于国际力量对比变化。全球治理体系是由全球共建共享的，不可能由哪一个国家独自掌握，全球治理结构如何完善应该由各国共同来决定。中国是现行国际体系的参与者、建设者、贡献者，是国际合作的倡导者和国际多边主义的积极参与者。中国要推动全球治理理念创新发展，积极发掘中华文化中积极的处世之道和治理理念同当今时代的共鸣点，努力为完善全球治理贡献中国智慧、中国力量。中国坚持从国情出发，坚持权利和义务相平衡，坚持发展中国家定位，

Promoting Global Governance Reform

At a meeting marking the 60th anniversary of the "Five Principles of Peaceful Coexistence" on June 28, 2014, Xi Jinping highlighted the need to reform global governance in response to new changes in international power dynamics. As we face a wider array of global challenges, it is ever more necessary to enhance and reform global governance. In addition to addressing existing challenges, such reform is critical to reshaping the international order and setting its rules and direction.

It is about how countries are positioned and expected to play their roles under an international order and an international institutional framework from a long-term perspective. A global governance structure is underpinned by power dynamics at the international level. Its reform is necessitated by changes in global power relations. The governance structure should be jointly built by all countries for the benefit of all, rather than dominated by any one country. Global consultation is necessary to decide how to improve this structure.

China participates in and contributes to the existing international order, promotes international cooperation and multilateralism, and actively participates in multilateral initiatives. Our willingness to contribute to the

把维护中国利益同维护广大发展中国家共同利益结合起来。保持开放、透明、包容姿态，同二十国集团各成员加强沟通和协调，共同把二十国集团维护好、建设好、发展好，促使二十国集团顺利完成从危机应对机制向长效治理机制转变，巩固其作为全球经济治理主要平台的地位。

innovative development of the concept of global governance is rooted in our culture, one that advocates a positive approach to life and proactive governance philosophy. We are ready to share our thoughts and do what is needed to help improve global governance.

Based on its prevailing national conditions as a developing country, China will seek the right balance between rights and obligations, and protect its own national interests in conjunction with the shared interests of other developing countries. We will pursue an open, transparent and inclusive process to strengthen consultation and coordination with other G20 members, to make the G20 framework more responsive and more relevant, and to ensure its successful transition from a crisis management mechanism to a major platform for global economic governance.

坚定不移全面从严治党，不断提高党的执政能力和领导水平

Exercising Strict Governance over the Party and Improving the Party's Ability to Govern and Lead

新时代党的建设总要求

中国特色社会主义进入新时代，中国共产党一定要有新气象新作为。中国共产党要团结带领人民进行伟大斗争、推进伟大事业、实现伟大梦想，必须毫不动摇坚持和完善党的领导，毫不动摇把党建设得更加坚强有力。中共十九大报告提出新时代党的建设总要求，即坚持和加强党的全面领导，坚持党要管党、全面从严治党，以加强党的长期执政能力建设、先进性和纯洁性建设为主线，以党的政治建设为统领，以坚定理想信念宗旨为根基，以调动全党积极性、主动性、创造性为着力点，全面推进党的政治建设、思想建设、组织建设、作风建设、纪律建设，把制度建设贯穿其中，深入推进反腐败斗争，不断提高党的建设质量，把党建设成为始终走在时代前列、人民衷心拥护、勇于自我革命、经得起各种风浪考验、朝气蓬勃的马克思主义执政党。这个总要求明确了新时代党的建设的根本原则、指导方针、鲜明主线、基本途径、总体布局、战略任务、

General Guidelines for Party Building for a New Era

As socialism with Chinese characteristics has entered a new era, our Party must have a new look and make new accomplishments. For the Party to unite the people and lead them in carrying out our great struggle, advancing our great cause, and realizing our great dream, we must unwaveringly uphold and improve Party leadership and make the Party stronger.

The report to the 19th CPC National Congress lays out general guidelines for Party building for a new era, calling for:

• upholding and strengthening the Party's leadership role, and ensuring effective governance within the Party and effective enforcement of Party discipline;

• strengthening the Party's long-term governance capacity, and preserving its forward-looking vision and its purity;

• raising political awareness, and reaffirming the Party's ideals, convictions, and purpose;

• tapping into the enthusiasm and innovative potential among the Party's rank and file;

• pursuing an integrated approach to raising political awareness, strengthening the Party's theoretical basis, improving its organizational structures, promoting ethical

根本目标，提出了党的建设的一系列新思想新论断新举措，开辟了马克思主义党建理论的新境界，是坚定不移推进全面从严治党的行动纲领和基本遵循。

standards, enforcing discipline, and enhancing institution building; and

• combating corruption as part of the effort to improve the efficacy of Party building, so as to build a Marxist governing party with a vibrant organizational culture, a party that is always ready to answer the call of the times, enjoys the support of the people, has the courage to reform itself, and is able to withstand all tests.

These guidelines provide clear direction, guidance and fundamental principles for Party building activities in a new era, and specify measures and strategic tasks to achieve our objectives. They embody our Party's new thinking on leadership, and represent a new chapter in Marxist theory on party building. They provide a basic framework for enforcing strict Party discipline.

打铁必须自身硬

2012年11月15日，习近平在人民大会堂同采访十八大的中外记者见面时，提出“打铁还需自身硬”。党的十九大报告进一步提出“打铁必须自身硬”。中国共产党在中国执政，就是要带领人民把国家建设得更好，让人民生活得更好。要肩负起这个使命，中国共产党就必须加强自身建设，保持自身的先进性和纯洁性，保持同人民群众的血肉联系，不断提高领导水平和执政水平，不断提高拒腐防变和抵御风险能力，不断提高科学执政、民主执政、依法执政水平，更好为人民服务。不全面从严治党，党就做不到“打铁必须自身硬”，也就难以发挥好领导核心作用。“打铁必须自身硬”，硬就硬在中国共产党人有着坚定的理想信念。中国特色社会主义进入新时代，中国共产党一定要有新气象新作为。党要团结带领人民进行伟大斗争、推进伟大事业、实现伟大梦想，必须毫不动摇坚持和完善党的领导，毫不动摇把党建设得更加坚强有力。

"It Takes a Good Blacksmith to Make Good Tools"

This expression was used by Xi Jinping on November 15, 2012, while he was being interviewed by domestic and international journalists covering the 18th CPC National Congress. As the governing party, the CPC must lead the people in building a better country and enable the people to live better lives.

To take on this mission, the Party must strengthen itself, maintain its own advanced and incorruptible nature, maintain its flesh-and-blood ties with the people, constantly elevate its leadership and administrative standards, constantly improve its ability to resist corruption and risks, and constantly strengthen its ability to administer scientifically, democratically and in accordance with the law, so as to serve the people better.

Unless it comprehensively exercises strict self-governance, the Party cannot be the "good blacksmith" who "makes good tools," and it will be unable to play its core leadership role. The "blacksmith" refers to the CPC, and the quality required comes from the firmly held ideals and beliefs of Party members. "It takes a good blacksmith to make good tools" is a solemn commitment made by the Party to the people.

保持战略定力

战略定力说的是领导者需要具备的一种能力和素养，一种工作和思维方法。简单地说，就是要有长远战略眼光，处乱不慌，沉得住气，不能急于求成，不能朝令夕改。习近平第一次使用战略定力这个词，是在2012年中央经济工作会议上，此后他又多次强调。领导人之所以提出这个要求，是因为中国经济发展已经进入新常态，对新常态的认识和实践刚刚起步，有的方面还没有破题，需要广泛探索，同时，中国也面临着日益复杂的国际环境，在今后较长时期内将面临重大外部挑战。保持战略定力，最核心的要求就是集中精力办好自己的事，稳字当头，稳中求变，稳中求进，推动中国经济走出一条质量高、效益好、结构优的发展新路，不断提升综合国力。

Maintaining a Strategic Focus

The ability to keep a strategic focus is an indispensable leadership quality. Simply put, it entails a strategic long-term perspective to guard against any distraction in the face of unforeseen challenges or any urge to embrace unrealistic quick solutions or frequent changes of course. Xi Jinping referred to the importance of a strategic focus for the first time at the Central Economic Work Conference in 2012, and has since reiterated it on multiple occasions.

A strategic focus is especially important in addressing emerging challenges, including long-term challenges, brought about by China's new normal in economic growth, which calls for new thinking and a series of new pilot programs, as well as by an increasingly complicated international environment.

A strategic focus is informed by an unwavering determination to stay on track toward our strategic goals. It provides ballast to ensure that reform moves proceed without disrupting economic and political stability. It helps propel our efforts to carve a new path to greater prosperity with a focus on the quality and efficiency of the implementation of our development strategies and on structural transformation.

发扬钉钉子精神

2013年2月召开的中共十八届二中全会上，习近平首次对钉钉子精神进行了详细阐述：我们要有钉钉子的精神，钉钉子往往不是一锤子就能钉好的，而是要一锤一锤接着敲，直到把钉子钉实钉牢，钉牢一颗再钉下一颗，不断钉下去，必然大有成效。如果东一榔头西一棒子，结果很可能是一颗钉子都钉不上、钉不牢。此后习近平多次强调钉钉子精神。

钉钉子精神要求真抓实抓，要求做实做细做好各项工作，所蕴含的是知行合一、务实重行的精神，攻坚克难、敢于担当的精神。“发扬钉钉子的精神”既是一种工作方法，更是一种工作态度。

Promoting the Spirit of Perseverance

Xi Jinping first highlighted the importance of perseverance at the second plenary session of the 18th CPC Central Committee in February 2013. He compared this quality to what is required to drive nails. More often than not, you cannot drive a nail into its right place in one go. Effective nailing requires repeated precision hammering. And to put your project in place, you have to repeat the same process of precision hammering many times. Failing that, you will end up with a shoddy project that is likely to fall apart any time. Since that meeting, Xi has on many occasions emphasized the virtue of perseverance.

Perseverance requires a combination of a pragmatic and down-to-earth approach to tackling challenges and a keen understanding of any underlying problems and the larger context. It is a mindset that is key to overcoming heavy odds and winning an uphill battle. Having the perseverance to hammer away until a task is done – This is one way of conduct and a clear-cut attitude to work.

党的政治建设

党的政治建设是党的根本性建设，决定党的建设方向和效果。党的十九大报告第一次将政治建设纳入党的建设总体布局，并强调以政治建设为统领，把党的政治建设摆在首位，突显政治建设的极端重要性。党的政治建设的主要内容包括：坚持党中央权威和集中统一领导，在政治上思想上行动上同党中央保持高度一致；制定和执行党的政治路线和方针政策、决策部署；严格遵守党的政治纪律和政治规矩；尊崇党章，认真学习、严格遵守党章；加强和规范党内政治生活，增强党内政治生活的政治性、时代性、原则性、战斗性；完善和落实民主集中制，既充分发扬民主，又善于集中统一；发展积极健康的党内政治文化，营造风清气正的良好政治生态；加强党性锻炼，不断提高政治能力和政治觉悟等等。在新时代党的建设总体布局中，党的政治建设是最重要的，居于统领、核心地位，同时又与其他各项建设

Raising Political Awareness Among Party Members

Raising political awareness is key to Party building, and will shape the direction and determine the effectiveness of our Party building efforts. It was included for the first time in the overall plan for Party building in the report to the 19th CPC National Congress, as a primary task of overriding importance. It requires, among others, the following actions:

• upholding the authority and centralized leadership role of the Central Committee, and always following its guidance;

• formulating and implementing the Party's political directives and guidelines, and making strategic decisions;

• enforcing Party discipline, especially as it relates to political issues;

• promoting respect for, awareness of, and strict adherence to the Party Constitution;

• enforcing a code of conduct for intra-party political life, and ensuring that intraparty activities respond to political challenges, reflect today's realities, and are principled and effective;

• improving the system of democratic centralism to ensure a right balance between democracy and centralism;

• developing within the Party a positive and healthy political culture that promotes

相互贯通、密切联系。党的政治建设抓好了，可以对党的其他建设起到纲举目张的作用。

integrity and ethical conduct; and

• strengthening Party members' sense of Party identity, raising their political consciousness, and improving their ability to handle political issues.

Raising political awareness among Party members is central to our Party building for a new era. It interacts with and is closely related to other Party development measures. Success in raising political awareness will ensure effective implementation of other measures.

党的思想建设

党的思想建设是党的基础性建设，是党永葆先进性和纯洁性的重要法宝。它指中国共产党为保持自己的创造力、凝聚力和战斗力而在思想理论方面所进行的一系列工作。思想建设的基本要求是用马克思列宁主义、毛泽东思想、邓小平理论、“三个代表”重要思想、科学发展观、习近平新时代中国特色社会主义思想武装全党，不断改造和克服党内一切非无产阶级思想，其实质是坚持马克思主义的思想领导，保证全党在思想上政治上行动上的高度一致，保持党的先进性和纯洁性。加强党的思想建设，要把坚定理想信念作为首要任务，教育引导全党加强党性修养，解决好世界观、人生观、价值观这个“总开关”问题，自觉做共产主义远大理想和中国特色社会主义共同理想的坚定信仰者和忠实实践者。党的十八大以来，全党开展了党的群众路线教育实践活动、“三严三实”专题教育、“学党章党规、学系列讲话、做合格党员”学习教育，成为党的思想建设的

Party's Ideological Work

Strengthening the Party's ideological work is vital to preserving the Party's forward-looking vision and its purity. It helps the Party realize its own innovative potential, provides cohesion, and strengthens the Party's ability to address ideological issues.

Strengthening the Party's ideological work entails effective implementation within the Party of principles of Marxism-Leninism, Mao Zedong Thought, Deng Xiaoping Theory, the Theory of Three Represents, the Scientific Outlook on Development, and Xi Jinping Thought on Socialism with Chinese Characteristics for a New Era. It requires resolve to overcome any tendencies incompatible with Marxist thinking. Its essence is adherence to Marxist philosophy, so as to preserve the Party's forward-looking vision and its purity, and ensure a high level of consistency in all Party activities, including on the ideological or political front.

Efforts in this connection include educational outreach that helps Party members stay true to the Party's ideals and convictions, strengthen their sense of Party identity, have a better understanding of the world around them and the meaning of life, and embrace communist values, so that they are better prepared to pursue communist ideals and socialism with Chinese characteristics.

Since the 18th CPC National Congress,

重要实践和有力抓手。党的十九大报告指出，要继续推进“两学一做”学习教育常态化制度化，在全党开展“不忘初心、牢记使命”主题教育。

a series of educational outreach initiatives focused on putting theory into practice have been launched, including activities to see members command and act on the Party's mass line, and a campaign for the observance of the Three Stricts and Three Earnests. We have regularized and institutionalized the requirement for all Party members to have a solid understanding of the Party Constitution, Party regulations, and related major policy addresses and to meet Party standards.

The report to the 19th CPC National Congress underlined the continued importance of these studies and related discussions and the need for them to be embedded into the Party's regular education programs to ensure that Party members will remain true to our original aspiration and keep our mission firmly in mind.

党的组织建设

党的组织建设是党的建设主要内容之一，主要包括党的组织制度建设、组织体系建设、干部队伍建设、党员队伍建设和民主集中制建设等内容。党要实现各个历史时期的政治任务，必须始终把加强党的组织建设摆在突出位置。党的干部是党和国家事业的中坚力量，干部队伍建设在党的组织建设中居于核心地位。党的十九大报告指出，要坚持党管干部原则，坚持德才兼备、以德为先，五湖四海、任人唯贤，事业为先、公道正派，落实好干部标准，建设高素质专业化干部队伍。要坚持党管人才原则，聚天下英才而用之，加快建设人才强国。党的基层组织是党的全部工作和战斗力的基础，基层组织建设是党的组织建设的基础性工作。党的十九大报告专门强调，要把基层党组织建设成为宣传党的主张、贯彻党的决定、领导基层治理、团结动员群众、推动改革发展的坚强战斗堡垒。党员队伍建设是党的组织建设

Improving the Party's Organizational Structures

Improving the Party's organizational structures is an important component of our Party building initiative. It encompasses development and improvement of rules and regulations, improvement of institutional arrangements, leadership development, membership development, and improvement of the system of democratic centralism. Enhancing the Party's organizational structures has always been important to accomplishing the Party's political tasks during different historical periods. Our team of Party officials are a central pillar of strength for our Party and our country, and leadership development should be front and center in our Party development efforts.

The report to the 19th CPC National Congress emphasized the need for the Party's supervision over its officials, and for development of a set of standards that ensure selection of officials on the basis of integrity, competence, dedication to service, and honesty regardless of where they are from, so as to build a team of high-caliber public servants.

It is critical to ensure the Party's leadership role in talent management. No effort will be spared to attract talent from far and near

的重要内容。党员是党的肌体的细胞和党的活动的主体，党员队伍建设是党的建设基础工程。党的十九大报告对新时代党员发展教育管理工作提出了新要求。

and make China a talent-strong country.

The Party relies on its organizations at local levels to ensure effective implementation of its objectives. It is therefore important to strengthen these organizations.

The report to the 19th CPC National Congress underlined the pivotal role of local-level Party organizations in communicating the Party's messages, implementing its decisions, overseeing community-level social governance, and mobilizing the people in a joint effort to pursue reform and development.

Membership development is an important aspect of our policy for enhancing the Party's organizational structures, and provides a basis for other Party development activities, as membership is what constitutes the fabric of the Party. The report to the 19th CPC National Congress articulated new guidelines for membership development and related educational outreach in a new era.

党的作风建设

作风建设是管党治党的永恒课题。党的作风是党的各级组织和全体党员在实践过程中形成的比较稳定的、反映党的特征和品格的整体精神风貌，包括党的思想作风、工作作风、领导作风、学风和生活作风等。党的作风就是党的形象，关系人心向背，关系党的生死存亡。中国共产党历来高度重视作风建设，在长期不懈奋斗中形成了一整套优良作风，突出表现为理论联系实际、密切联系群众、批评与自我批评三大作风，以及谦虚谨慎、不骄不躁和艰苦奋斗等作风。党的十九大报告强调，加强作风建设，必须紧紧围绕保持党同人民群众的血肉联系，增强群众观念和群众感情，不断厚植党执政的群众基础。凡是群众反映强烈的问题都要严肃认真对待，凡是损害群众利益的行为都要坚决纠正。坚持以上率下，巩固拓展落实中央八项规定精神成果，继续整治“四风”问题，坚决反对特权思想和特权现象。重点强化政治纪律和组织纪律，带动廉洁纪律、群众纪律、工作纪律、生活纪律严起来。坚持

Promoting Ethical Standards Within the Party

Promoting ethical standards is a perennial theme associated with intra-party governance. Ethical conduct is expected of Party organizations at all levels and of all Party members all the time. It shows who we are and what we are striving for. It is reflected in our political discussions, in the performance of duties, in the exercise of authority, in our pursuit of knowledge, and in our daily lives. Adherence to ethics rules is vital to our Party's reputation, to the level of public support we enjoy, and, indeed, to the Party's survival.

The CPC has always attached great importance to ethics issues. Over a long period of time, our Party has demonstrated a high level of ethics and integrity, distinguished, in particular, by an emphasis on putting theory into practice, a people-centric mindset, and a readiness for criticism and self-criticism, in addition to modesty, prudence, aversion to arrogance and recklessness, and a hardworking spirit.

The report to the 19th CPC National Congress reaffirmed the importance of enforcing ethical standards, strengthening the Party's close ties with the people, always bearing in mind the interests and aspirations of the people, and building public support. Resolute and effective measures will be taken to address major

开展批评和自我批评，坚持惩前毖后、治病救人，运用监督执纪“四种形态”，抓早抓小、防微杜渐。赋予有干部管理权限的党组相应纪律处分权限，强化监督执纪问责。加强纪律教育，强化纪律执行，让党员、干部知敬畏、存戒惧、守底线，习惯在受监督和约束的环境中工作生活。

concerns among the public and any irregularities that undermine the people's interests.

Party officials should lead by example in further implementing the Party Central Committee's Eight-point Decision on Improving Party and Government Conduct on the basis of what we have achieved in this connection. Our campaign to fight unhealthy behaviors and tendencies will continue, targeting, in particular, obsession with formalities instead of substance, too much red tape, indulgence in pleasure, a penchant for extravagance, and privilege seeking in all its forms and expressions. Discipline must be enforced at both political and organizational levels, to help promote integrity and ethical behavior in our interaction with the public, in the performance of official duties, and in our daily lives.

Criticism and self-criticism continue to be a valuable tool for identifying and addressing inadequacies or transgressions. Oversight and enforcement could lead to disciplinary or legal action, including an oral warning, a written censure, a demotion, or prosecution, and help stop an emerging problem from metastasizing into a crisis. The Party's supervisory organs will be authorized to take disciplinary action as necessary, and enforce compliance accountability. Training on the importance of discipline will be expanded, and discipline enforcement strengthened, so as to ensure respect for and strict adherence to laws and regulations, and create an environment in which submission to oversight and constraints becomes the order of the day.

党的纪律建设

党的纪律是党的各级组织和全体党员必须遵守的行为规则，是维护党的团结统一、完成党的任务的保证。中国共产党是靠革命理想和铁的纪律组织起来的马克思主义政党，纪律严明是党的光荣传统和独特优势，加强纪律建设是全面从严治党的治本之策。2013年1月，在十八届中央纪委二次全会上，习近平明确提出“加强党的纪律建设”。党的十九大把纪律建设纳入新时代党的建设总体布局，是习近平新时代中国特色社会主义思想中关于党的建设思想的重要理论和实践创新。加强党的纪律建设，必须把纪律挺在前面，坚持纪严于法、纪在法前，重点强化政治纪律和组织纪律，带动廉洁纪律、群众纪律、工作纪律、生活纪律严起来。必须加强纪律教育，制定完善纪律规定，强化纪律执行，坚持开展批评和自我批评，坚持惩前毖

Strengthening Party Discipline

Party organizations at all levels and all members must obey Party rules and regulations. Discipline is vital to the unity of the Party, and provides a basis for realizing the Party's objectives.

The CPC is a Marxist party informed by revolutionary ideals and iron discipline. The latter has been an important feature of our glorious tradition and our unique strength. Discipline enforcement is therefore pivotal to improving governance within the Party.

At the second plenary session of the 18th CPC Central Commission for Discipline Inspection in January 2013, Xi Jinping called for strengthening Party discipline. The issue of discipline was included in an overall plan for Party development for a new era at the 19th CPC National Congress. An emphasis on Party discipline as part of the Party building initiative is an innovative, important component of Xi Jinping Thought on Socialism with Chinese Characteristics for a New Era.

To strengthen Party discipline, we must put discipline front and center, ensuring that the Party's rules and regulations are more rigorous and demanding than laws. Discipline must be enforced at both political and organizational levels, to help promote integrity and ethical behavior in our interaction with the

后、治病救人，运用好监督执纪“四种形态”，让党员、干部知敬畏、存戒惧、守底线。

public, in the performance of official duties, and in our daily lives. Training on the importance of discipline will be expanded; rules and regulations improved; and discipline enforcement strengthened. Criticism and self-criticism continue to be a valuable tool for identifying and addressing transgressions and preventing their future occurrence. Oversight and enforcement will be stepped up, and disciplinary or legal action will be taken whenever necessary, including an oral warning, a written censure, a demotion, or prosecution, so as to ensure respect for and strict adherence to laws and regulations.

党的制度建设

制度建设是具有根本性、全局性、稳定性和长期性的重大问题。党的制度建设是指党在长期领导工作和党内生活中形成的党的组织和党的成员必须共同遵守的党内法规、条例、规则等。党内制度建设，既是党的建设的一个重要方面，也是党的各项基础建设的关键环节。党的制度建设通过对各项工作制度化、规范化，形成党的一系列规章制度，从而为党的其他方面的建设提供基本遵循和制度保障。党的十九大报告强调把制度建设贯穿党的各项建设之中，回归了制度建设的内在规律性，更加凸显了制度建设的重要地位和作用。推进全面从严治党，必须坚持制度治党、依规治党，把权力关进制度的笼子，用制度管权、管事、管人。加强党的制度建设，必须建立健全以党章为根本、民主集中制为核心的党内法规制度体系，扎紧制度笼子；必须强化制度宣传教育，增强全党制度意识，筑牢制度治党的思想基础；

The Party's Institutional Development

Institutional development is a long-term, all-encompassing endeavor of vital importance that provides stability and continuance.

Encompassing development of rules and regulations that guide the Party's exercise of leadership, as well as intra-Party activities, it is an important aspect of Party development, and vital to other Party development activities. It provides an institutional framework with a complete set of norms and directives to guide all programs and initiatives.

The report to the 19th CPC National Congress reiterated the imperative to enhance institutional development, its vital importance, and the need to incorporate it in all Party building activities. Enforcing strict Party discipline requires developing rules and regulations, and confining the exercise of power within an institutional cage. All organs, activities and officials are subject to institutional oversight and constraints without exception.

Institutional development must be focused on developing an intra-Party framework of rules and regulations on the basis the Party Constitution and the principles of democratic centralism, with the aim of tightening institutional constraints. Educational outreach must be expanded to raise the awareness

必须严格执行制度，坚持制度面前人人平等、制度执行没有例外，增强党内法规制度执行力，使制度成为“硬杠杠”“高压线”。

of the importance of institutional oversight and constraints, and to help strengthen the theoretical basis for institutional development. Accountability enforcement must be enhanced, and the principle of equality before the rules and regulations in effect must be applied to all with no exception. Clear lines that can never be crossed will be established to ensure the effectiveness of accountability enforcement.

把权力关进制度的笼子

2013年1月，习近平在十八届中央纪委二次全会上强调，要加强对权力运行的制约和监督，把权力关进制度的笼子里，形成不敢腐的惩戒机制、不能腐的防范机制、不易腐的保障机制。制度问题更带有根本性、全局性、稳定性、长期性。用制度管权，就是要把权力关进制度的笼子里。把权力关进制度的笼子里，首先要建好笼子。要抓住治权这个关键，编密扎紧制度的笼子，按照决策、执行、监督既相互制约又相互协调的原则区分和配置权力，构建严密的权力运行制约和监督体系。要让人民监督权力，努力形成科学有效的监督体系，增强监督合力和实效。要让权力在阳光下运行，推进权力运行公开化、规范化，完善党务公开、政务公开、司法公开和各领域办事公开制度。要建立权力清单、实行权责对应，坚持有权就有

Confining the Exercise of Power Within an Institutional Cage

Xi Jinping introduced the idea of an "institutional cage" at the second plenary session of the 18th CPC Central Commission for Discipline Inspection in January 2013. He said that the move to confine the exercise of power within an institutional cage is meant to strengthen scrutiny of the work and deter possible misuse of power by officials. It entails establishing a mechanism that prevents, deters and punishes corruption.

Institutions are of fundamental, overall, and long-lasting importance, and have a profound impact on the stability of the country. To check the exercise of powers, there must be a solid cage of institutions. Administration holds the key to this goal. Powers should be properly designated so that making, execution, and supervision of decisions will check each other and coordinate with each other, and a system of institutions operates effectively to check and oversee the exercise of power.

The people should be granted powers of scrutiny as part of the efforts to build a sound mechanism for supervision with effective synergy. Powers must be exercised in the light of day, and this exercise of power should be procedure-based and made public.

责，失职要问责。要反对特权思想、特权现象，决不允许以权谋私，决不允许搞特权。

Party affairs, government operations, judicial affairs, and other affairs in relevant areas will be made more transparent. Lists of powers will be defined, so that powers and responsibilities are matched, and those exercising power bear correspondent responsibilities and are held accountable for any abuse. Any ideas and practices redolent of privilege will be opposed, and it is absolutely forbidden to seek privilege or to abuse one's power for personal gain.

深化政治巡视

巡视制度是中国共产党党内的一项重要制度，是指中央和省、自治区、直辖市党委，通过建立专门巡视机构，按照有关规定对下级党组织领导班子及其成员进行监督的制度。2003年，以党内法规的形式把巡视制度确定为党内监督的十项制度之一；2007年，党的十七大把巡视制度写入党章；2009年，党中央颁布《中国共产党巡视工作条例（试行）》；2015年8月，中共中央印发《中国共产党巡视工作条例》；2017年5月，中央政治局审议了《关于修改〈中国共产党巡视工作条例〉的决定》，并于7月1日正式颁布。按照规定，巡视工作坚持中央统一领导、分级负责；坚持实事求是、依法依规；坚持群众路线、发扬民主；开展巡视工作的党组织承担巡视工作的主体责任；巡视组的主要工作职责是

System of Political Inspection

Inspection is an important means of conducting oversight inside the CPC. The Central Committee and the Party committees of provinces, autonomous regions, and municipalities directly under the central government all have special organs through which to conduct inspections of the leading bodies and members of the Party organizations under their jurisdiction.

The system of inspection became one of the ten systems of intra-Party supervision in 2003; the system was included in the Constitution of the CPC at the 17th National Congress of the CPC in 2007; the Regulations on Inspection of the CPC (trial) were promulgated by the Central Committee in 2009; the Regulations on Inspection of the CPC were promulgated by the Central Committee in August 2015; and in May 2017, the Political Bureau of the Central Committee reviewed the Decision on Revising the Regulations on Inspection of the CPC, which was promulgated on July 1.

The Central Committee commands the overall work of inspection, and Party organizations at different levels hold corresponding responsibilities. Inspections are conducted based on facts and in accordance with the laws and regulations. The Party's mass line

对下级党组织领导班子及其成员进行监督；巡视的方式有专项巡视、“回头看”、“机动式”巡视等。十八大以来，中央一共组织了12轮巡视，巡视利剑作用彰显，实现中央和省级党委巡视全覆盖。实践证明，巡视制度是有效的、管用的。巡视工作成为党风廉政建设和反腐败斗争的重要平台，是党内监督和群众监督相结合的重要方式，是上级党组织对下级党组织监督的重要抓手，为全面从严治党提供了有力支撑。

and democracy are followed. The Party organizations that conduct such inspections hold the primary responsibility. Inspection teams supervise the leading bodies and members of the Party organizations at lower levels, and they conduct special inspections, follow-up re-examinations, and random inspections if necessary.

Since 2012, the Central Committee has organized 12 rounds of inspection, covering all the Party organization above provincial level. Disciplinary inspections have cut like a blade through corruption and misconduct. They have become an effective way to massively improve Party conduct, uphold integrity, and combat corruption. Integrating intra-Party oversight and public supervision, they serve as an important channel for the Party organizations at higher levels to supervise their subordinate organizations, and contribute to the Party's exercise of full and strict self-governance.

全面增强执政本领

党的十九大报告中指出，领导十三亿多人的社会主义大国，我们党既要政治过硬，也要本领高强。这是中国共产党站在新时代推进中国特色社会主义伟大事业高度，对提高党的政治能力和领导水平提出的新要求。全面增强执政本领的举措包括：增强学习本领，建设马克思主义学习型政党，推动建设学习大国；增强政治领导本领，科学制定和坚决执行党的路线方针政策，把党总揽全局、协调各方落到实处；增强改革创新本领，善于结合实际创造性推动工作，善于运用互联网技术和信息化手段开展工作；增强科学发展本领，善于贯彻新发展理念，不断开创发展新局面；增强依法执政本领，加快形成党内法规制度体系，加强和改善对国家政权机关的领导；增强群众工作本领，创新群众工作体制机制和方式方法，推动群团组织增强政治性、先进性、群众性；增强狠抓落实本领，坚持雷厉风行和久久为功相结合，以

Strengthening Governance Ability

To guide a large socialist country of more than 1.3 billion people toward prosperity, the CPC must demonstrate political strength and competence, which will be further tested as it promotes the great cause of socialism with Chinese characteristics for a new era.

Improving governance ability requires:

• embracing continuous learning, and building a Marxist party that values learning and a country that encourages learning;

• sharpening leadership skills, and developing and implementing guidelines and policies to ensure the Party's role of leadership and coordination in all areas;

• promoting reform and innovation, including applying innovation outcomes to practical projects and expanding the use of the internet and information technology;

• promoting evidence-based development to break new ground in development efforts by applying new thinking;

• enhancing rule-based governance, developing and improving the Party's rules and regulations, and strengthening leadership by the Party over government bodies;

• making greater efforts to engage with the people through innovative mechanisms, and promoting political consciousness among civil society actors, so that they will be in a

钉钉子精神做实做细做好各项工作；增强驾驭风险本领，健全风险防控机制，勇于战胜前进道路上的各种艰难险阻。

better position to play their role as progressive organizations, and better represent the people;

• improving effectiveness in implementing programs and projects, by combining speed with perseverance and meticulousness; and

• managing risks, by improving risk prevention and control mechanisms, and tackling challenges head-on.

“四个意识”

2016年1月29日，中共中央政治局会议首次公开提出增强政治意识、大局意识、核心意识、看齐意识这“四个意识”。思想上的统一、政治上的团结、行动上的一致是中国共产党的事业不断发展壮大的根本所在。这么大一个党、一个国家，没有集中统一，没有党中央坚强领导，没有强有力的中央权威，是不行的、不可想象的。中国共产党领导是中国特色社会主义制度的最大优势，加强党的领导关键是坚持党中央集中统一领导。只有增强政治意识、大局意识、核心意识、看齐意识，自觉在思想上政治上行动上同以习近平同志为核心的党中央保持高度一致，才能使党更加团结统一、坚强有力，始终成为中国特色社会主义事业的坚强领导核心。“四个意识”不能只停留在口头表态上，要切实落实到行动上。

"Four Consciousnesses"

On January 29, 2016, the Political Bureau of the CPC Central Committee publicly spelled out for the first time the "Four Consciousnesses": maintaining political integrity, thinking in terms of the big picture, following the leadership core, and keeping in alignment with the central Party leadership. Alignment in thinking, political unity and unison in action have been essential to the continuing development and growth of the CPC's endeavors. It would be unthinkable and unworkable for such a large Party and such a large nation to be without centralized unity, strong Party leadership, and powerful central authority.

The greatest strength of socialism with Chinese characteristics is the leadership of the Party, and the key to strengthening it is to maintain the centralized and unified leadership of the Party's Central Committee. The only way for the Party to become stronger and more united, and for it to always be the strong core leader of Chinese socialism, is for Party members to maintain political integrity, think in terms of the big picture, follow the leadership core, and keep in alignment with the central Party leadership, and for them to always be aware of staying in close unison in both thoughts and deeds with the Party Central Committee with Xi Jinping at its core. These "Four Consciousnesses" cannot be given lip service – they must be implemented in actions.

严明党的政治纪律和政治规矩

中国共产党作为马克思主义政党，讲政治是突出的特点和优势。党的政治纪律是指各个不同时期根据党的政治任务的要求，对各级党组织和党员的政治活动和政治行为的基本要求，是各级党组织和党员在政治生活中必须遵守的行为准则。政治纪律的基本要求是：各级党组织和党员，必须在政治原则、政治立场、政治观点和路线、方针、政策上同党中央保持高度一致。2015 年 1 月 13 日，习近平在十八届中央纪委第五次全会上正式提出了“政治规矩”一词。党内规矩是党的各级组织和全体党员必须遵守的行为规范和规则。党的规矩包括：其一，党章是全党必须遵循的总章程，也是总规矩。其二，党的纪律是刚性约束，政治纪律更是全党在政治方向、政治立场、政治言论、政治行动方面必须遵守的刚性约束。其三，国家法律是党员、干部必须遵守的规矩，法律是党领导人民制定的，全党必须模范执行。其四，党在长期实践中形成的优良传统和工

Strict Political Discipline and Political Rules of the Party

Taking a clear political stand is the outstanding characteristic and strength of the CPC as a Marxist party. The Party's political discipline refers to the basic requirements that Party organizations and Party members must follow in their political activities and conduct in different periods of time, as required by the Party's political tasks at that time. Every Party organization and every Party member must follow the Central Committee regarding political principles, stance, views, lines and policies.

Addressing the fifth plenary session of the 18th CPC Central Commission for Discipline Inspection on January 13, 2015, Xi Jinping coined the term "political rules."

The intra-Party rules are the rules and code of conduct that every CPC organization and every CPC member must observe. They include, *inter alia*:

• the Constitution of the Communist Party of China, which is the overriding statute that the whole Party must observe;

• Party discipline, which is mandatory and binding, requiring all members of the Party to strictly abide by the guidelines and principles of the Party when making speeches or taking actions of a political nature;

作惯例，也需要很好地遵守。在所有党的纪律和规矩中，第一位的是政治纪律和政治规矩。

• state laws, to which no CPC member or official is exempt. As the Party has led the people in enacting the state laws, all CPC members must set an example in observance of the law; and

• the great traditions and working practices developed by the Party over the years, which must be maintained.

Among all Party discipline and Party rules, political discipline and political rules are the supreme criterion of surmounting importance.

中央八项规定

2012年12月4日，中共中央政治局召开会议，确定了关于改进工作作风、密切联系群众的八项规定。主要内容是：改进调查研究，到基层调研要深入了解真实情况；精简会议活动，切实改进会风；要精简文件简报，切实改进文风；规范出访活动；改进警卫工作，坚持有利于联系群众的原则；改进新闻报道；严格文稿发表；厉行勤俭节约，严格遵守廉洁从政有关规定。八项规定既不是最高标准，更不是最终目的，只是中共改进作风的第一步，是共产党人应该做到的基本要求。习近平要求，“各级领导干部要以身作则、率先垂范，说到的就要做到，承诺的就要兑现，

Eight-Point Decision on Improving Party and Government Conduct

The Eight-point Decision on improving Party and government conduct and building closer ties with the people was issued at a meeting of the Political Bureau of the CPC Central Committee on December 4, 2012. It covers the following main areas:

• doing better research and analysis and truly understanding actual conditions when doing grassroots-level studies;

• streamlining meetings and improving the way meetings are conducted;

• making documents and briefing papers more concise and improving writing styles;

• standardizing procedures for working visits abroad;

• improving security guard work and continuing to observe the principle of doing what improves relations with the people;

• improving news report;

• having strict rules on the publication of articles; and

• promoting frugality and the strict observance of rules on incorruptibility in government.

The Eight-point Decision is neither the highest standards, nor the ultimate one. It is only the first step in the CPC's efforts to improve its practices – the minimum expected

中央政治局同志从我本人做起。”中央八项规定之后，一系列关于作风建设的措施陆续出台。

of Party members. Xi Jinping stated that "leading officials at all levels must lead by example and serve as role models, they must do as they say and live up to their promises. Within the Political Bureau, I will start with myself." Following the release of the Eight-point Decision on Improving Party and Government Conduct, a series of measures on work practices are being issued.

反对“四风”

2013年6月，习近平在党的群众路线教育实践活动工作会议上指出，党内脱离群众的现象大量存在，集中表现在形式主义、官僚主义、享乐主义和奢靡之风这“四风”上。我们要对作风之弊、行为之垢来一次大排查、大检修、大扫除。“四风”是违背中国共产党的性质和宗旨的，是当前群众深恶痛绝、反映最强烈的问题，也是损害党群干群关系的重要根源。反对“四风”时，要从群众最关心、最迫切的问题入手，着力解决关系群众切身利益的问题，解决群众身边的不正之风问题，把改进作风成效落实到基層，真正让群众受益，努力取得人民群众满意的实效。

Eliminating the "Four Malfeasances"

During a work conference in June 2013, on the campaign to educate Party members about the mass line, Xi Jinping pointed out that there were numerous instances of the Party losing its connection with the people. These were manifested in the "Four Malfeasances": going through the motions, excess bureaucracy, self-indulgence and extravagance. We must undertake a major clean-up of the negative effects of these phenomena.

The "Four Malfeasances" are contrary to the nature and mission of the CPC. They are detested by the people and provoke the strongest feelings, and they are a major cause of damage to relations between the Party and the people. Their elimination must start with those issues of greatest concern and greatest urgency to the people. Efforts should focus on inappropriate conduct which directly touches on the people; the impact of improvements should reach all the way to the grassroots and let the people truly feel the benefits, and we must work for results which satisfy the people.

党的群众路线教育实践活动

开展党的群众路线教育实践活动是中共十八大作出的一项战略决策。活动从2013年6月开始，2014年10月基本结束，以为民、务实、清廉为主要内容，在全党范围内自上而下分两批开展。通过开展这次活动，广大党员、干部受到马克思主义群众观点的深刻教育，形式主义、官僚主义、享乐主义和奢靡之风得到有力整治，恢复和发扬了批评和自我批评优良传统，以转作风改作风为重点的制度体系更加完善，影响群众切身利益的症结难点得到突破，党的执政基础更加稳固。

The Campaign to Educate Party Members About the Mass Line

The CPC made a strategic decision at its 18th National Congress to launch a campaign to educate Party members about the mass line. The campaign started in June 2013, and was basically concluded by October 2014. It was mainly about serving the people, being pragmatic and being incorruptible, and took place throughout the entire Party from the top down in two phases. This campaign gave Party members and officials a deeper understanding of the Marxist perspective on working with the people; it made effective inroads against the "Four Malfeasances;" and it revived and encouraged the great traditions of criticism and self-criticism. It refined institutional systems by focusing on changing work practices, led to breakthroughs in critical issues directly affecting the interests of the people, and further strengthened the foundation of the Party's governance.

“三严三实”专题教育

“三严三实”是习近平对各级领导干部改进作风提出的要求，即严以修身、严以用权、严以律己，谋事要实、创业要实、做人要实。2015年4月19日，中共中央办公厅印发了《关于在县处级以上领导干部中开展“三严三实”专题教育方案》，对2015年在县处级以上领导干部中开展“三严三实”专题教育作出安排。严以修身，就是要加强党性修养，坚定理想信念，提升道德境界，追求高尚情操，自觉远离低级趣味、自觉抵制歪风邪气。严以用权，就是要坚持用权为民，按规则、按制度行使权力，把权力关进制度的笼子里，任何时候都不搞特权、不以权谋私。严以律己，就是要心存敬畏、勤于自省，遵守党纪国法。谋事要实，就是要从实际出发谋划事业和工作，使点子、政策、方案符合实际情况、符合客观规律、符合科学精神，不好高骛远，不脱离实际。创业要实，就是要脚踏实地、真抓实干，敢于担

Special Education Program of the Three Stricts and Three Earnests

The Three Stricts and Three Earnests were expectations of leading officials at all levels set by Xi Jinping. They call upon officials to be strict with themselves in self-cultivation, using power, and exercising self-discipline; and to be earnest in one's thinking, work, and behavior when performing official duties, taking initiatives, and interacting with others. On April 19, 2015, the General Office of the CPC Central Committee issued the "Program for Educating Leading Officials at the County Level and Above on the Three Stricts and Three Earnests," and made plans for its implementation in 2015.

Strict in self-cultivation means enhancing Party members' awareness of the Party's expectations, firmly supporting their ideals and beliefs, raising their ethical standards, pursuing noble values, self-consciously avoiding vulgarity, and consciously resisting unhealthy practices and negative influences.

Strict in using power means always using power to serve the people, always exercising power according to rules and institutional procedures, keeping the power within the confines of an institutional cage, and

当责任，勇于直面矛盾，善于解决问题，努力创造经得起实践、人民、历史检验的实绩。做人要实，就是要做老实人、说老实话、干老实事。通过专题教育，推动了政治生态改善，使全面从严治党的氛围更加浓厚、领导干部的标杆作用更加明显。

never seeking special privileges or using it for personal gain.

Strict in exercising self-discipline means holding in awe and veneration, being diligent in self-examination and strictly abiding by Party discipline and state laws.

Earnest in one's thinking when performing official duties means basing plans on reality, so that ideas, policies and programs are appropriate to actual conditions, accord with objective laws and the scientific spirit, and are neither overly ambitious nor detached from reality.

Earnest in one's work when taking initiatives means being firmly grounded, taking real action, daring to be held accountable, confronting problems directly, being adept at solving them, and striving to produce results that are workable, acceptable to the people and can stand the test of time.

Earnest in one's behavior when interacting with others means being an honest person who speaks and acts honestly.

This special education program improved the political environment, fostered a more intense atmosphere of strict Party self-governance, and better leveraged the role of leading officials.

“两学一做”学习教育

2016年2月，中共中央决定在全体党员中开展“两学一做”学习教育，以“学党章党规、学系列讲话，做合格党员”为主要内容，以尊崇党章、遵守党规为基本要求，以用习近平系列重要讲话精神武装全党为根本任务，强调“基础在学、关键在做”，着力解决党员队伍在思想、组织、作风、纪律等方面存在的突出问题。2017年3月，中办印发了《关于推进“两学一做”学习教育常态化制度化的意见》，持续推动全面从严治党突出“关键少数”并向基层延伸，使“两学一做”成为党员教育的基本内容。开展“两学一做”学习教育，是加强中国共产党思想政治建设的一项重大部署，是面向全体党员深化党内教育的重要实践，是推动全面从严治党向基层延伸的重要举措。十九大报告指出，推进“两学一做”学习教育常态化制度化，以县处

"Two Studies and One Action" Education Campaign

In February 2016, the CPC Central Committee decided to start a campaign to educate all Party members in the "Two Studies and One Action." The education campaign asked all Party members "to study the Party Constitution and rules, and speeches of Xi Jinping, and to become qualified Party members."

Its basic requirement was that Party members respect the Party Constitution and obey its rules, and that the entire Party takes its essential task to be drawing spiritual strength from Xi Jinping's most important speeches. In stressing that "the prerequisite is study, and the key is action," it focused on resolving some of the major ideological, organizational, behavioral and disciplinary problems among Party members.

In March 2017, the General Office of the CPC Central Committee distributed its "Opinion on Institutionalizing Education on the 'Two Studies and One Action.'" It will target the "key few" officials at important positions and extend this work to the grassroots, while continuing to comprehensively promote strict Party self-governance, and make the "Two Studies and One Action" part of the basic education of Party members. Promoting such

级以上领导干部为重点，在全党开展“不忘初心、牢记使命”主题教育，用党的创新理论武装头脑，推动全党更加自觉地为实现新时代党的历史使命不懈奋斗。

education is an important part of the plan to strengthen Party ideology, an important way for the Party to reinforce internal Party education for its members, and an important measure for extending comprehensive strict Party self-governance down to the grassroots.

The 19th CPC National Congress pointed out that we would launch a campaign on the theme of "staying true to our founding mission" to enable all Party members, especially officials at and above the county and director level, to arm themselves with the Party's new theories and become more purposeful in working tirelessly to accomplish the Party's historic mission in the new era.

新时期好干部标准

2013年6月28日，习近平总书记在全国组织工作会议上，提出了“好干部”的“五条标准”：即信念坚定、为民服务、勤政务实、敢于担当、清正廉洁。信念坚定，要求不断加强党性修养，时刻用党章、用中共党员标准要求自己，树立正确的世界观、人生观、价值观，坚定共产主义远大理想，为中国特色社会主义而奋斗。为民服务，要求密切联系群众，深入基层、深入实际、深入群众，想问题、做决策、干工作，都要以人民群众为导向，时刻践行全心全意为人民服务的宗旨，并以此为标准衡量自己所作所为的价值所在。勤政务实，要求认真学习马克思主义理论特别是中国特色社会主义理论体系，丰富知识储备，完善知识结构，打牢履职尽责的知识基础；同时，必须求真务实、真抓实干，着力解决群众最关心、反映最强烈的问题。敢于担当，要求坚持原则、认真负责，敢于担负重任，敢于进行改革创新，身先士卒、率先垂范，为人民群众的利益牺牲自己。清正廉洁，要求时刻自省自励，老实做人，踏实做事，清白为

Standards for Good Officials for a New Era

At a national meeting on organizational work on June 28, 2013, Xi Jinping summarized five standards to assess good officials: They must be firm in their ideals and convictions, be committed to serving the people, be diligent in work, be ready to take on responsibilities, and be clean and upright.

Being firm in their ideals and convictions requires that Party officials have a strong sense of Party principles, always check themselves against the Party constitution and the norms for Party members, embrace a correct worldview, outlook on life and values, cherish the ideals of communism, and strive to work for socialism with Chinese characteristics.

Being committed to serving the people means that they maintain close ties with the people, learn about the true conditions of the people, take a people-oriented approach in handling problems and making decisions, fulfill the Party mission of serving the people wholeheartedly, and check all their actions against this set of standards.

Being diligent in work requires Party officials to learn Marxist theory, especially theories on socialism with Chinese characteristics, and enrich their knowledge in order to better perform their duties. They must also be dedicated to their work in a down-to-earth,

官，永葆共产党员的纯洁本色，做到高压线不碰、红线不越、底线不丢。上述五条标准在近年来得到了很好地贯彻，中国的选人用人状况和风气明显好转。

realistic and pragmatic manner, and tackle the problems that concern the people most and prompt the strongest public reaction.

Being ready to take on responsibilities reflects Party officials' adherence to principles, sense of responsibility, courage to take on heavy tasks, initiative to reform, innovation, setting a personal example, and willingness to sacrifice themselves to the interests of the people.

To remain clean and upright, Party officials have to often engage in self-examination, be honest in their conduct, be down-to-earth in their work, maintain their integrity as Communists, and never cross the line of Party discipline.

Through commitment to these standards, the process of selecting and appointing officials has improved in recent years.

反腐败无禁区、全覆盖、零容忍

勇于自我革命，从严管党治党，是中国共产党最鲜明的品格。党的十八大以来，面对纷繁复杂的国际国内形势和千头万绪的各个领域工作，以习近平同志为核心的党中央始终把党要管党、从严治党的政治责任牢牢扛在肩上，始终以强烈的历史责任感、深沉的使命忧患感和顽强的意志品质，旗帜鲜明推进党风廉政建设和反腐败斗争，坚持无禁区、全覆盖、零容忍，严肃查处腐败分子，坚决遏制腐败现象蔓延势头，着力营造不敢腐、不能腐、不想腐的政治氛围。

A Zero-Tolerance Anti-Corruption Campaign That Knows No Bounds

Courage to reform itself and enforce strict discipline is the CPC's most distinctive characteristic. In response to complex domestic and international challenges and needs in an evolving context, the Central Committee with Xi Jinping at its core has launched a sweeping campaign against corruption since the 18th CPC National Congress. The campaign is premised on the imperative that the Party must supervise itself and enforce strict discipline and ethical standards. Vital to the Party's political mandate, its historic mission and goals, and, indeed, its survival, no place has been out of bounds, no ground left unturned, and no tolerance shown in the fight against corruption. It will serve as a powerful deterrent against corruption, and help create an environment that encourages integrity and removes incentives for corruption.

坚定不移"打虎""拍蝇""猎狐"

"老虎"喻指位居高层的腐败官员，"苍蝇"指身处基层的腐败官员，"狐狸"则指一些涉嫌犯罪的外逃国家工作人员和重要腐败案件涉案人。在中国，不得罪腐败分子，就要得罪13亿人民。党的十八大以来，以习近平同志为核心的党中央以巨大的政治勇气和历史担当，密集"打虎"全覆盖、中国反腐无禁区，零容忍"拍蝇"不手软、清理群众身边的腐败，海外"猎狐"追逃追赃、天罗地网肃清"避罪天堂"，交出沉甸甸的成绩单。

Taking Firm Action to "Take Out Tigers," "Swat Flies," and "Hunt Down Foxes"

If we do not fight corruption, we will do a disservice to the 1.3 billion Chinese people. Since the 18th CPC National Congress, the Central Committee with Xi Jinping at its core has launched a sweeping, zero-tolerance campaign against corruption with great courage as part of the effort to accomplish the Party's historic mission. The fight against corruption knows no bounds and leaves no ground uncovered. It targets "tigers" (corrupt senior officials), "flies" (corrupt low-ranking bureaucrats) and "foxes" (fugitives abroad suspected of major economic crimes), and aims to shut down all safe havens for criminals, wherever they are. Impressive success has been achieved in this campaign.

赢得反腐败斗争压倒性胜利

在中国，人民群众最痛恨腐败现象，腐败是中国共产党面临的最大威胁。只有以反腐败永远在路上的坚韧和执着，深化标本兼治，保证干部清正、政府清廉、政治清明，才能跳出历史周期率，确保党和国家长治久安。党的十九大报告指出，当前，反腐败斗争形势依然严峻复杂，巩固压倒性态势、夺取压倒性胜利的决心必须坚如磐石。要坚持无禁区、全覆盖、零容忍，坚持重遏制、强高压、长震慑，坚持受贿行贿一起查，坚决防止党内形成利益集团。在市县党委建立巡察制度，加大整治群众身边腐败问题力度。不管腐败分子逃到哪里，都要缉拿归案、绳之以法。推进反腐败国家立法，建设覆盖纪检监察系

Securing a Sweeping Victory in the Fight Against Corruption

Corruption is what the people resent most; and it is the greatest threat to our Party. Fighting corruption requires resolve and perseverance, and it should be an on-going process with no end point. Not only should we confront corruption's symptoms, we must also tackle its root causes. Only by promoting integrity and ethical conduct among officials, and building a clean government and a clean political environment, can we break the cycle of corruption and ensure long-term stability of our Party and our country.

As stated in the report to the 19th CPC National Congress, the fight against corruption remains an uphill battle, and we must not waver in our resolve to build on the overwhelming momentum and secure a sweeping victory. This fight knows no bounds, and will leave no ground uncovered and show no mercy. Effective constraints, tough measures and long-term deterrence are essential in this connection, in order to target both those who take bribes and those who offer them, and prevent the emergence of special interests within the Party.

Regular disciplinary inspections will be undertaken by Party committees at the municipal or county level in an intensified effort to

统的检举举报平台。强化不敢腐的震慑，扎牢不能腐的笼子，增强不想腐的自觉，通过不懈努力换来海晏河清、朗朗乾坤。

address corruption that occurs on the doorstep of local residents. Wherever offenders flee, they will be brought back to justice. A national anti-corruption bill is under consideration, and a corruption reporting platform is being developed to allow cases to be reported to both disciplinary inspection commissions and oversight agencies.

Deterrence against corruption will be strengthened, and the institutional cage fortified, to provide a shield against corruption temptation, and help create a political environment as clean as a pristine river.

图书在版编目（CIP）数据

中国关键词．十九大篇：全二册：汉英对照／中国外文出版发行事业局，当代中国与世界研究院，中国翻译研究院著；蔡力坚，韩清月译．-- 北京：新世界出版社，2018.12（2021.4 重印）

ISBN 978-7-5104-6664-9

Ⅰ．①中… Ⅱ．①中… ②当… ③中… ④蔡… ⑤韩… Ⅲ．①中国特色社会主义－社会主义建设模式－研究－汉、英②中共十九大（2017）－学习参考资料－汉、英 Ⅳ．①D616 ②D229

中国版本图书馆 CIP 数据核字（2018）第 284040 号

中国关键词：十九大篇（汉英对照）

作　　者：中国外文出版发行事业局　当代中国与世界研究院
中国翻译研究院

翻　　译：蔡力坚　韩清月

审　　定：徐明强

改　　稿：David W. Ferguson［英］

责任编辑：闫传海

特约编辑：杨星宇

责任印制：王宝根

出版发行：新世界出版社

网　　址：http://www.nwp.com.cn

社　　址：北京西城区百万庄大街 24 号（100037）

发 行 部：(010) 6899 5968（电话）　(010) 6899 0635（电话）

总 编 室：(010) 6899 5424（电话）　(010) 6832 6679（传真）

版 权 部：+8610 6899 6306（电话）　nwpcd@sina.com（电邮）

印　　刷：天津旭非印刷有限公司

经　　销：新华书店

开　　本：880mm × 1230mm　1/32　尺寸：95mm × 200mm

字　　数：100 千字　　印　张：15

版　　次：2018 年 12 月第 1 版　2021 年 4 月第 2 次印刷

书　　号：ISBN 978-7-5104-6664-9

定　　价：78.00 元（全二册）